ENCOUNTER WITH MYSTERY

ENCOUNTER WITH MYSTERY

❊❊

*Reflections on L'Arche
and living with disability*

Edited by
FRANCES YOUNG

DARTON · LONGMAN + TODD

First published in 1997 by
Darton, Longman and Todd, Ltd
1 Spencer Court,
140–142 Wandsworth High Street
London SW18 4JJ

ISBN 0–232–52232–4

A catalogue record for this book is available from the British Library

The Scripture quotations used are, unless otherwise indicated, from the New
Revised Standard Version of the Bible.

Designed by Sandie Boccacci
Photoset in 10.5/13.5 Adolee Caslon by Intype London Ltd
Printed and bound in Great Britain by
Redwood Books, Trowbridge, Wiltshire

CONTENTS

Part II
REFLECTIONS ON L'ARCHE AND ITS SIGNIFICANCE FOR THE CHRISTIAN TRADITION

Part III
SHARERS AND CARERS THINK THEOLOGICALLY

THE CONTRIBUTORS

Frances Young, the book's editor, is the mother of Arthur, a young man with severe mental and physical disabilities. She holds the Edward Cadbury Chair of Theology in the University of Birmingham and is a Methodist minister. She is the author of *Face to Face: A Narrative Essay in the Theology of Suffering*.

Jean Vanier is the founder and continuing leader and inspirer of the L'Arche communities. He is a lay Roman Catholic, a leader of retreats and the author of many books, such as *Community and Growth*, *The Broken Body*, *Jesus the Gift of Love*, *Our Journey Home*.

Gilles Le Cardinal teaches at the Université de Technologie de Compiègne, while being a facilitator to the L'Arche communities.

Gilbert Adam became a priest in the Roman Catholic Church after living in the L'Arche community, and is now priest and chaplain in Trosly-Breuil.

Gerard Daucourt is Roman Catholic Bishop of Troyes, and formerly worked at the Secretariat for Christian Unity in Rome, where he also served as the priest of Il Chicco, the L'Arche community.

Ronan Sharkey lives in the L'Arche community at Trosly-Breuil with his family, and teaches at the Université de Technologie de Compiègne.

David Ford is Regius Professor of Divinity in the University of Cambridge, and a lay Anglican.

Youakim Moubarac was a Lebanese Roman Catholic priest who participated in the first meeting at L'Arche, Trosly, but has since died.

Mark Santer is the Anglican Bishop of Birmingham.

Nicholas Peter Harvey is a lay Roman Catholic theologian and writer, known for his books, *Death's Gift* and *The Morals of Jesus*.

A. M. (Donald) Allchin is an Anglican priest and Honorary Professor in the University of Wales, Bangor, known for his writings on spirituality and theology, and a long-time friend of L'Arche in Britain.

Simon Horne is an Anglican curate in Basingstoke and part-time research student at the University of Birmingham working on a thesis concerning biblical images of impairment. He is married to Mel, who was also a participant in the second meeting at Trosly-Breuil, bringing experience of her own physical impairment into the discussions.

John Goldingay is David Allan Hubbard Professor of Old Testament Studies at Fuller Theological Seminary, Pasadena. He was formerly Principal of St John's College, Nottingham (Anglican). He attended the first meeting with his wife, Ann, who has multiple sclerosis.

Ian Cohen is an Anglican priest in Oxfordshire, and father of Ben, a profoundly disabled young man with severe epilepsy.

INTRODUCTION

When we enter the world as new-born babies, the first thing we do is cry. No one worries about that. It's natural and necessary in order to expand the lungs and begin the breathing process. Crying is essential to life. It's ordinary. There's nothing tragic about it.

But that's the first and last time people find crying easy to accept. Things that make you cry become unacceptable – whether they be suffering and hurt, disappointment or disability, they are seen as tragic, and thus problematic. Theology has been obsessed with theodicy throughout the modern period. This book challenges that perspective.

Those who have contributed to this collection of essays have all discovered that physical or mental impairment – indeed, fragility and dependence, and having to deal daily with the demands of bodiliness – may turn out to be creative. They can create a space which is holy, a desert place where one meets God, and therefore reaches an understanding of the truth about the human condition.

For some contributors, the catalyst has been the life of the L'Arche communities; for others it has been living as carers – as parents or husbands. But L'Arche generated this work. L'Arche began when Jean Vanier took two people to live with him as friends, two people who had spent their lives in an institution for the mentally handicapped, as they were then generally called. In the village of Trosly-Breuil there are now many houses (known as *foyers*) making up a larger community centred on the L'Arche community church – a converted barn. Gradually community houses have been formed around the world, dedicated to shared living with the poorest and most vulnerable people in our societies. Jean himself has written much that is known and valued ecumenically. But the story of this book began when Jean asked Donald Allchin and me to collaborate with him in gathering a group of theologians to reflect on, and think through, the implications of the values and lifestyle of L'Arche.

The immediate genesis of the book was the second meeting, in November 1995. At the first meeting, two years earlier, the group had shared personal testimonies and had experienced, for just a weekend (and for most of us for the first time), something of the life of L'Arche at Trosly-Breuil, where it all began. That meeting was remarkably generative, and all the participants felt privileged to have been members. As one put it:

> During this weekend there was an intensification of thought due to those who could not articulate thought. L'Arche, and the other sources of testimony to suffering, make greater, not lesser, demands on thought – thought that engages with and becomes immersed in feeling, imagination, action, indignity, and lack of control.

Jean was seeking ways to communicate the treasure given to L'Arche – though another participant responded:

> I would like to speak not only about treasure but about 'mystery'. One cannot tell people about a mystery, as theologians write about God. A mystery is communicated by participation. That, I believe, is why several of us stressed the contemplative dimension of our experience of visiting L'Arche. We found ourselves drawn into mystery. The quality of attention to the Lord communicates itself, simply by being what it is. 'The light shines in the darkness', and it shines by shining.

One aspect of this was the 'extraordinary power that the gathering around broken minds and bodies has to overcome, undermine or relativise barriers'. Some found themselves in contemplative mode; others noted a quality of listening never before experienced among academics; another said he had worshipped and prayed in a way not possible for a long while. We were 'putting the mind into the heart', and vice versa.

One fruit of that first gathering was the emergence of a collection of 'sayings' – what, among the Desert Fathers, would have been known as 'apophthegmata', wise words. These were circulated anonymously, and represent a distillation of the memory of that first encounter. A selection is worth quoting:

> 'Community means you never suffer alone.'
> 'Brokenness is one of God's greatest gifts; it is the key to accepting human brokenness and the brokenness of the Church.'
> 'What is really human is the capacity to ask for help, and that is the gift of the unlikely givers.'
> '*Moi tout seule ne pas capable*' ('Me, alone, can't do it.')
> 'I smile. Therefore, you are.'
> 'I need to be loved by somebody with skin on.'
> 'The greatest problem is when people behave as if you are not there.'
> 'This is a privileged desert.'
> 'They [persons with mental disabilities, the poor] have the capacity to evangelise us [the intelligent, priests, etc.].'
> 'My saviour is the one who needs me.'
> 'In creation there is fragility and vulnerability: that is the nature of creation.'
> 'We need the stranger; we lack the very people we are afraid of because they are different.'
> 'Christian faith is not problem-solving but mystery-encountering.'

The climax of that first meeting, at least for me, was that shift in perspective, the discernment that, theologically speaking, we had to move away from problem-solving to mystery-encountering. Here lay the genesis of a new endeavour – to address the doctrines of Christian belief from the perspective of L'Arche and see what was revealed; to let L'Arche open our eyes to the traditions of Christian worship and spirituality; to let L'Arche break down the barriers in an ever-widening ecumenical embrace. At the second meeting some of us tried out the first versions of these essays; others were stimulated into writing something to add; others not at the second meeting were invited to share in our enterprise. Now we wish to share our experience and our thinking – for we have not only discovered that testimony is the most fundamental form of theology, but we also believe that we are touching the heart of Christianity in a way which is both ecumenical and true to the tradition.

There are two difficult matters which, as a group, we need to comment on at the start.

1. We are conscious of the problem of 'us' talking about 'them' – and this despite the fact that many at L'Arche, Trosly-Breuil, speak of 'them' as 'the poor', and so reinforce the unhappy picture of 'us' doing good to 'them'. (This rhetoric certainly links the neediness of persons with mental disabilities into the traditions of a certain kind of Roman Catholic spirituality, but to the English ear it runs the risk of sounding patronising, or possibly invoking liberation theology in an inappropriate way.) We know as a group that what has enriched us and the L'Arche tradition is in fact a sense of mutuality and reciprocity, of belonging to one another – and some of us are disturbed by the implication of 'difference'. Yet others of us know that, as carers, we have had no choice, confronted as we are by the differences – between the child who leaves to live their own life and the child who remains dependent into adulthood; or between the competent, professional marriage-partner and the different person, with increasing disabilities, who has become life's companion. Yet others feel that they are privileged onlookers, neither being members of L'Arche, nor sharing the demands and responsibilities of care. In the end, we can only speak from where we are. Nor should we dismiss the importance of 'competent us' receiving from, and being ministered to by, those we thought we were there to help and assist. The paradox of mutuality may arise from naming the difference.

2. 'Political correctness' has alerted some of us to the delicacies of

how we are to name that difference. It is important for many people that they are accepted first as persons – persons who happen to have learning difficulties. It is important for people with physical impairments that the disabilities which society, in its organisation and priorities, adds to their problems are properly attributed, and that responsibility is acknowledged. But for myself, I have to say that to describe my son as having learning difficulties is meaningless: I have learning difficulties myself – I've never felt so incompetent as the evening I spent in a L'Arche *foyer* almost unable to make myself understood because of my inability to express myself adequately in French. But there was that other L'Arche *foyer* where language was irrelevant – as it is with my son. He has made me competent, through years of practice, in non-verbal communication, in communion and togetherness beyond words, in smiles and touch. Yet I need to name the difference between us – and if the word 'handicap' is now contentious, I need to state that he has profound mental and physical disabilities. Others in this volume use the language they find the most natural, and we beg our readers to understand, and to look beyond the words we use to the mystery we mean.

Each of us has our own voice, our own context and our own discourse. There has been no attempt to harmonise; we simply invite the reader to find their own level, to sample and to dip, reading what interests them or challenges their thinking. Introductory paragraphs are provided so as to assist the process of selection. Part I of this book lets different people within L'Arche (often in translation from the French) speak of their encounters with mystery, and of their challenge to contemporary society. Part II lets visitors from outside respond to L'Arche as revelatory, as the place where truths within the Christian tradition are refreshed for our time. Part III brings together the theological reflections of carers and sharers, people whose personal journey has often been through loss, but whose vision has been renewed – not least through L'Arche. All of us offer an invitation to a new perspective: one where crying is not the end of the world but the beginning of new life; where death is the essential prelude to resurrection; where the desert proves to be the place of truth, the holy place where we encounter our selves, others and God.

Frances Young
Summer 1996

CHARTER OF THE COMMUNITIES OF L'ARCHE

L'Arche began in 1964 when Jean Vanier and Father Thomas Philippe, in response to a call from God, invited Raphael Simi and Philippe Seux, two men with mental handicaps, to come and share their life in the spirit of the gospel and of the Beatitudes that Jesus preached.

From this first community, born in France and in the Roman Catholic tradition, many other communities have developed in various cultural and religious traditions.

These communities, called into being by God, are united by the same vision and the same spirit of welcome, of sharing and simplicity.

I. Aims

1. The aim of L'Arche is to create communities which welcome people with a mental handicap. By this means L'Arche seeks to respond to the distress of those who are too often rejected, and to give them a valid place in society.
2. L'Arche seeks to reveal the particular gifts of people with a mental handicap who belong at the very heart of their communities and who call others to share their lives.
3. L'Arche knows that it cannot welcome everyone who has a mental handicap. It seeks to offer not a solution but a sign – a sign that a society, to be truly human, must be founded on welcome and respect for the weak and the downtrodden.
4. In a divided world, L'Arche wants to be a sign of hope. Its

communities, founded on covenant relationships between people of differing intellectual capacity, social origin, religion and culture, seek to be a sign of unity, faithfulness and reconciliation.

II. Fundamental principles

1. Whatever their gifts or their limitations, people are all bound together in a common humanity. Everyone is of unique and sacred value, and everyone has the same dignity and the same rights. The fundamental rights of each person include the rights to life, to care, to a home, to education and to work. Also, since the deepest need of a human being is to love and to be loved, each person has a right to friendship, to communion and to a spiritual life.

2. If human beings are to develop their abilities and talents to the full, realising all their potential as individuals, they need an environment that fosters personal growth. They need to form relationships with others within families and communities. They need to live in an atmosphere of trust, security and mutual affection. They need to be valued, accepted and supported in real and warm relationships.

3. People with a mental handicap often possess qualities of welcome, wonderment, spontaneity and directness. They are able to touch hearts and to call others to unity through their simplicity and vulnerability. In this way they are a living reminder to the wider world of the essential values of the heart, without which knowledge, power and action lose their meaning and purpose.

4. Weakness and vulnerability in a person, far from being an obstacle to union with God, can foster it. It is often through weakness, recognised and accepted, that the liberating love of God is revealed.

5. In order to develop the inner freedom to which all people are called, and to grow in union with God, each person needs to have the opportunity of being rooted and nourished in a religious tradition.

III. The communities

1. Communities of faith

1. L'Arche communities are communities of faith, rooted in prayer and trust in God. They seek to be guided by God and by their weakest members, through whom God's presence is revealed. Each community member is encouraged to discover and deepen his or her spiritual life and live it according to his or her particular faith and tradition. Those who have no religious affiliation are also welcomed and respected in their freedom of conscience.

2. Communities are either of one faith or inter-religious. Those which are Christian are either of one Church or interdenominational. Each community maintains links with the appropriate religious authorities and its members are integrated with local churches or other places of worship.

3. Communities recognise that they have an ecumenical vocation and a mission to work for unity.

2. Called to unity

1. Unity is founded on the covenant of love to which God calls all the community members. This implies welcome and respect for differences. Such unity presupposes that the person with a handicap is at the centre of community life.

   This unity is built up over time and through faithfulness. Communities commit themselves to accompany their members (once their membership is confirmed) throughout their lives, if this is what those members want.

2. Home life is at the heart of a L'Arche community. The different members of a community are called to be one body. They live, work, pray and celebrate together, sharing their joys and their suffering and forgiving each other, as in a family. They have a simple lifestyle which gives priority to relationships.

3. The same sense of communion unites the various communities throughout the world. Bound together by solidarity and mutual commitment, they form a worldwide family.

3. Called to growth

1. L'Arche communities are places of hope. Each person according to his or her own vocation, is encouraged to grow in love, self-giving and wholeness, as well as in independence, competence and the ability to make choices.
2. The communities wish to secure for their members education, work and therapeutic activities which will be a source of dignity, growth and fulfilment for them.
3. The communities wish to provide their members with the means to develop their spiritual life and to deepen their union with and love of God and other people.
4. All community members are invited to participate, as far as possible, in decisions concerning them.

4. Integrated in society

1. L'Arche communities are open and welcoming to the world around them. They form an integral part of life in their localities, and seek to foster relationships with neighbours and friends.
2. The communities seek be competent in all the tasks they are called to accomplish.
3. The communities wish to enable people with a handicap to work, believing work to be an important means of integration.
4. The communities seek to work closely with:

   - the families and guardians of people who are handicapped,
   - professionals,
   - government authorities,

   and with all those who work in a spirit of justice and peace for people who are handicapped.

IV. Conclusion

L'Arche is deeply concerned by the distress of people who suffer injustice and rejection because they are handicapped. This concern should impel the communities of L'Arche to do all they can to defend the rights of people with a mental handicap, to support the creation of places of welcome for them, and to call on our society to become more just and respectful towards them.

The communities of L'Arche want to be in solidarity with the poor of the world, and with all those who take part in the struggle for justice.

❧ Part I ❧

Voices
from within
L'Arche

❦ 1 ❦

L'ARCHE – A PLACE OF
COMMUNION AND OF PAIN

JEAN VANIER

*In order to explain how the community of L'Arche generates new under-
standings of spirituality, Jean Vanier tells something of his own story and
of how L'Arche came about. He explores the mystery of the broken,
vulnerable heart, and the importance of revealing to those who are hurt
their own preciousness. This can only happen through communion. But
communion with 'the stranger' reveals one's own inner darkness and
woundedness. The strong are taught by the weak what the love of Jesus is:
'Jesus is like a child or a beggar, inviting us, asking us, begging us, to open
our hearts to let him in, so that he may reveal his glory in our fragile
beings.' So barriers are broken down.*

Not long ago there was a meeting of a group of competent and
organised people who wanted to start a L'Arche community in their
city. The conversation or discussion was interesting, intellectual,
sometimes heated, sometimes seriously pragmatic. Shortly before
the end of the meeting, 20 men and women with mental handicaps
from a near-by institution came into the room. They walked up to
each person, embraced them, asked them their name and entered
into a heartfelt, simple conversation with each one. The atmosphere
in the room was instantly transformed. Those competent, organised
people started to smile and laugh, and to return the kisses. They
entered fully into this heartfelt conversation.

I find that so often people with handicaps have this strange power
to transform a rather tense, intellectual and serious atmosphere into
one of fun, joy and relaxation, where people no longer hide their

hearts behind masks of knowledge and power, but become themselves. ⸙

Six years ago, we welcomed Antonio into one of our homes in my own L'Arche community. He had lived in a psychiatric hospital for 20 years. Antonio is now 26; he cannot speak, or use his hands or legs. He is fragile, vulnerable and totally dependant on others. He has also a malformation in the thorax which means that he needs constant oxygen. However, there does not seem to be any rebellion or depression in Antonio, though he can become peeved from time to time. Antonio seems to have accepted his situation. If you come near him and call him by name, he looks at you with trust and love, a smile fills his face and his eyes shine.

The astonishing thing about Antonio is his influence upon those 'assistants' who come to live with him. Most of the assistants are Christian, but when they first arrive they often know little about their faith; they come seeking community. If you ask them about their life in L'Arche, many will tell you that Antonio has changed their lives:

> I come from a competitive and conflict-ridden world. I was taught to hide my weaknesses and limits behind a mask, and to be strong and aggressive in order to win in studies, work and sport, in order to climb the ladder of promotion. Antonio is leading me into another world, a world of love and tenderness where we respect one another, need one another, live in communion one with another; a world where we try to help each other to use our gifts, to grow humanly and spiritually, and to find our place in the body of community.

Living with Antonio, feeding him and bathing his fragile body day after day, clothing him in his littleness, helplessness and trust, calls forth qualities in the heart of others. Listening to his non-verbal language, and trying to understand his pain and needs, helps people lower their barriers and calls them into a communion of the heart which has a transforming effect.

How is it that this little, fragile man – who, not too long ago, would have been refused eucharistic communion, and who many today see as a burden, with no human value – how is it that he can have such a powerful effect on people who accept him and see him as a human person? We are beginning to experience the truth of Paul's words:

> But God chose what is foolish in the world to shame the wise; God chose what is weak in the world to shame the strong; God chose what is low and despised in the world, things that are not. (1 Cor. 1:27)

God seems to have chosen Antonio for a special mission of love in our world today. He is revealing a presence of God which Jesus announced: ' "Whoever welcomes this child in my name welcomes me, and whoever welcomes me welcomes the one who sent me" ' (Luke 9:48). In and through Antonio, Jesus is calling assistants to love, to compassion and to freedom. Are those who are rejected and scorned able to become the healers of those who reject them and who are governed by prejudice?

In this paper I would like to explore some of the areas of spirituality and theology that have been opened up to me as I live in community with people who have mental handicaps, and as I discover what a gift they are to me as well as to others.

My own journey

Let me begin by saying something about my own personal journey and vocation. I was in the Navy for eight years. I left the Navy in 1950 to follow Jesus. Years of searching and of formation began. I lived in a small community in France founded by Father Thomas Philippe, a Dominican priest. It had been founded for lay people who wanted to study philosophy and theology, and to live the gospel values of prayer, poverty and welcome of the poor. I completed a doctorate in philosophy and then started teaching. In 1963, Father Thomas became the chaplain for an institution of 30 men with mental handicaps. He had begun to discover the truth and the power of Paul's words quoted above.

These people who were fragile and vulnerable, whose reason had not developed fully, who had suffered rejection, seemed to be disposed in a special way to receive Jesus' message of love. Their minds were limited, but their hearts were open and crying out for love. This seemed to be the realisation of the parable of the wedding feast, to which good, important, capable and religious people are invited, but refuse the invitation because they are too taken up with their own projects. When the poor, the crippled, the lame and the blind are invited, they come running, with joy! (Luke 14:15–24) Father Thomas suggested that I come and visit his new friends who seemed particularly open and near to Jesus.

To cut a long story short, after meeting Father Thomas' new friends, I stopped teaching philosophy and started to visit different institutions and psychiatric hospitals, where hundreds of people were floundering in pain, rejection, oppression and horrible living conditions. Having lived with the 'winners' in society, I discovered the 'losers'. In 1964 I welcomed from one of these institutions Raphael Simi and Philippe Seux, two men with mental handicaps. They came to live with me in a small, rather broken-down house in Trosly-Breuil, a village in northern France, the same village where Father Thomas was living. This was the beginning of L'Arche.

The development of L'Arche

Thirty-three years later I am still living in L'Arche. The community has grown: there are now 400 people, 200 with mental handicaps and about 200 who have the privilege of living and working with them, creating family with them, in the name of Jesus. We live in small houses scattered in and around Trosly. Each household is like a family, a basic community, where each member has his or her place.

From this initial community in France, over 100 others have been born in different countries and cultures. Some of these communities are specifically Roman Catholic, some belong to a Protestant tradition, others are interdenominational, and a few are inter-religious. We welcome people with handicaps, essentially because they are in pain and because they have been rejected and seen as worthless, and not because of their religious affiliation. This has led us to the discovery of our common, broken humanity, and of God's love for each person whatever their origins or religious tradition may be.

During the early years of L'Arche, I began to discover the pain in the hearts of parents. So often they feel confused by, and even guilty in, the presence of their son or daughter who is different from other children. Frequently they find little support from their larger family or neighbours, and are left alone with their burden. Sometimes husbands leave their wives when they discover their child has a severe handicap: the mother is left alone to cope with a difficult situation. On some occasions parents, unable to cope, abandon their child to a hospital or institution: they feel ashamed. The discovery of this pain led Marie-Helen Mathieu and myself, in 1971, to found Faith and Light, a sister-organisation of L'Arche. Faith and Light groups are support communities, based on the gospel message, for people with mental handicaps, and for their parents and friends. They do not live together, but meet once or twice a month and sometimes for weekends, holiday camps, retreats and pilgrimages. There are now 1,300 Faith and Light communities in 70 countries. Each community brings together about 30 people to share and pray together, to celebrate life and to create a sense of belonging.

Faith and Light has transformed many parents. They discover a network of friends, a community adapted to their needs, where they can share their burdens with others and find loving support. They discover that their son or daughter is special to Jesus, that they have a gift of love. They are no longer alone, and no longer feel ashamed. They can celebrate life together. Their children with a handicap find young friends, and these friends discover in a living way the message of the Gospels.

The power to awaken and disturb

What exactly have Antonio, Philippe, Raphael and many others taught me? How have they been instruments of transformation for me? How have they led me to meet and love Jesus in a new way?

Living with Raphael and Philippe, I discovered the mystery of the broken, vulnerable heart. We can all understand the terrible pain of the broken dream when a mother gives birth to a child with a handicap. She was expecting a beautiful, healthy child; she discovers that her child will be different. A father once told me that his immediate reaction at the birth of his daughter was: 'What have I done to God that he should bring such a tragedy into my life?' So often there is a feeling of guilt hidden in parents.

If we can easily understand the pain of parents, many people do not realise the terrible pain in the child's heart – what it means for people to feel all their life that they have no value or are not wanted. Such children readily sense that they have always been a cause of pain and anguish for their parents. I gradually became aware of the pain, the loneliness and the feelings of guilt which were buried deep in the hearts of Raphael and Philippe. Guilt, because if people always seem to fear, reject and mock you, then little by little you become convinced that you are no good, that you are bad; that if people do not love you, it is because you are not lovable. The cry that flowed from the hearts of Raphael and Philippe was essentially a cry for love and for recognition.

As we lived together, I discovered in the Gospel of Luke a discreet invitation from Jesus:

> 'When you give a luncheon or a dinner do not invite your friends or your brothers or your relatives or rich neighbours, in case they may invite you in return, and you would be repaid. But when you give a banquet, invite the poor, the crippled, the lame, and the blind. And you will be blessed.' (Luke 14:12–14)

Jesus is asking us not just to eat together, but to befriend people with handicaps. This is the blessing we are living in L'Arche and in Faith and Light. In the Navy and when I studied philosophy and theology, I was rather austere, mainly preoccupied by my work and studies. I loved my profession. I always sought to do well and to be admired. When I look back now, I realise I was rather fearful of relationships. I would obey, command or teach – but personal relationships, and all the vulnerability that they imply, were difficult for me.

When I took Raphael and Philippe from the institution, I wanted to help them find life and dignity. In a way, it was easy for me to be generous and to do things for them. I was their 'superior', and could tell them what to do. Little did I realise that they were leading me into the mystery of communion that would gradually transform my life – just as Antonio has been transforming the lives of the many assistants who have lived with him.

I discovered that to love people is not first of all to *do* things *for* them but to *reveal* something to them. It is to reveal that they have a value, that they are beautiful and precious, that there is meaning to their lives. Their broken self-image is thus transformed into a more whole one. They find new confidence in themselves, and a desire to live and to grow. This is done through our being with them, enjoying their presence, listening to them, understanding their pain and their needs, becoming their friend and being vulnerable to them. A whole attitude of the heart is revealed through the eyes, the face, the smile and the whole body. Only when we become aware of that can we respond to the cry of their hearts

When we are generous, we are in a superior position; we remain on a pedestal. We do good to others. But when we enter into a personal relationship with another person, we live a communion of hearts. We become vulnerable one to the other, open to the other's pain. It is a heart-to-heart relationship which becomes a bond. This brings joy and celebration to both. The wounded person is no longer alone; the wound is transformed into dancing. When we are loved, we discover our beauty and value, which are much deeper than all that is broken in our lives. This communion is not possession; it is rather a love that empowers and liberates, calling the other to be truly him or her self and to develop his or her gifts. In L'Arche I discovered this communion as a gift of God, flowing from the heart of God. We no longer see people with handicaps as society sees them, but as God sees them.

Raphael and Philippe were unable to develop their intelligence and manual skills; they would never be able to become totally independent. Sickness had left each one with a real handicap. They were not looking for success or power, or to step up the ladder of human promotion as I had done. They were seeking something more fundamental to the human person: a communion of hearts which is the to-and-fro of love, where each one gives and each one receives, where each one is a source of joy for the other.

The cry in the hearts of Raphael, Philippe and many others was a call for me to conversion and to littleness. It was easy for me to be generous; it was much more difficult for me to become vulnerable, to lower the defence mechanisms around my heart, to welcome them as friends, to receive from them the gift of their hearts and their presence, and to live simply with them. That meant dying to my need for power and individual success.

Here we touch on the fundamental spirituality and pedagogy of L'Arche. It is not just good teaching, trying to make people as independent as possible – rather, it means entering into a relationship of friendship with each person so that together we can discover the joy and inner liberation that comes through belonging and growing towards greater maturity. This new family or community we are forming is not a family of flesh and blood, but is given by Jesus, calling us to a covenant of love; it does not want to be closed upon itself, but open and present to neighbours, to parishes and to society in general. Thus, people with handicaps can reveal their gift to all and be like yeast in the dough, affecting the whole neighbourhood.

Living with people who have handicaps has revealed to me the well, or deep source of love, within me – and my own yearning for communion. It has helped me to give space to others within me, to rest with them in love. It has also revealed all that is broken within me: my fears, anguish and darkness which are hidden behind barriers preventing the communion and littleness of love.

Peter's story

We welcomed Peter in 1978. He had a severe mental handicap and had always lived with his mother who understood his cries, his grunts, his smiles or expressions of anger. She loved him and he loved her. When he was 30, his mother had to be hospitalised and there was no way he could live alone. Peter was placed in another hospital, but this separation was totally incomprehensible to him. It brought him loneliness, insecurity, fear and anguish. Eventually he came to L'Arche. When I left the leadership of the community, I spent a year in his household. There were moments when he would scream and scream and scream. His anguish and inner pain awakened my own anguish and inner pain. I could not stand his cries of anguish which I could neither calm nor control. If I had been alone with him, not in community, I could have been tempted to hit him. I was terribly humiliated by my attitudes. It is not easy when your own violence is revealed to you, especially when you feel called by Jesus to reveal his love to the poor and to receive his love from them.

Shortly after this painful experience, I discovered a letter Carl Jung had written to a Christian woman. In reference to the text in Matthew 25:31–46, he expressed his admiration of Christians who saw a real presence of Jesus in the hungry, the thirsty, the sick, the imprisoned, the naked and the stranger. He was astonished, however, that they did not see Jesus in the hunger, thirst, poverty, sickness, imprisonment and nakedness of their own hearts. Could Jesus really be hidden in my own darkness, I wondered? I began to discover how the light of God is called to enter into darkness, that I must not hide or deny this darkness to myself or to others, pretending that I am part of an élite. I had to accept that I too am part of a terribly wounded humanity. How could I really accept the woundedness of Antonio and Peter if I was not accepting my own? I too needed help. I too needed to discover that I am loved by Jesus just as I am, with all that is broken in me, with all my fears, limitations, blockages and handicaps. As my barriers began to come down, I discovered a lot of anguish inside me which sprang from my early childhood. I had had to protect myself from this painful, chaotic world of guilt, fear and loneliness. This protection had soiled even the best motivations of love. I had had to protect myself from pain by finding pleasure in material or spiritual success, admiration and a positive self-image. It is not easy to go through the dark night in order to reach that source of love and of life which is deeper than all the anguish, in order to find the presence of our loving God.

Antonio led me into the tenderness and communion at the heart of my being. Peter showed me the violence within me. Both taught me truths about who I really am – beautiful yet chaotic. In each of us there are latent capacities to give life, as well as places of darkness and death, capable of sowing death. We often hide our darkness behind our capacities to win and be admired. To grow to maturity, it is important to recognise and accept who we are, to make the right choices and to find the help and spiritual nourishment we need in order to move from chaos and fear to compassion and communion. Both Antonio and Peter, and many others like them, have led me into the truths of the gospel and of my need for Jesus to enable me to become a man of communion and to accept with more humility all that is broken within me.

Open to the call of Jesus

In one of our communities, Peter spends a lot of time in the chapel of his house. One day an assistant asked him if he liked to pray. When he answered that he did, she asked: 'What do you do when you pray?' 'I listen', he replied. 'What does God say to you?', she asked. 'He says that I am his beloved son', was his reply.

Sometime ago a little girl with a handicap made her first communion. The Eucharist was beautiful and was followed by a little celebration with the family. At one moment the girl's uncle said to her mother: 'Wasn't it beautiful? It's too bad that she did not understand anything.' The little girl heard the remark and with tears in her eyes said: 'Don't worry, Mummy, Jesus loves me as I am'.

After a talk given by Gilbert, a priest, I asked Didier what had touched him the most. He replied: 'When Gilbert was speaking, my heart was burning'. I am sure that if I had asked Didier what Gilbert had said he would not have been able to tell me.

People who have developed minds often want ideas and knowledge about God. This helps them to be admired for their brilliance and spirituality. People with mental handicaps do not find pleasure in ideas about God; their joy is in living with Jesus, feeling he is close, knowing him as a friend. Their hearts are searching for love and for presence. That explains why they are open in a special way to Jesus, the Word made flesh, who is present among us, who came to reveal his friendship with each one of us.

In L'Arche and in Faith and Light, we are beginning to see the truth of Paul's words about the choice of God – that God chooses the weak, the foolish, the lowly and the despised. This does not mean that God has not chosen others who are wise and strong. It means that Jesus, the God of love, came to give himself to those who feel lonely and pushed aside, and who cry out for love, who are open and vulnerable to love, who let themselves be led by love. Jesus cannot give himself to those who are closed in on themselves and only want ideas about God. The wise and the rich must leave their securities, and their need for temporal and spiritual power and wealth, in order to discover Jesus, the lover. They must recognise their needs and poverty enough to open the doors of their hearts to receive him, to be led and taught by him.

God's weakness is stronger than human strength

The trust that flows from the littleness and helplessness of Antonio has awakened the hearts of many assistants. A strange power is hidden in children, in sick people, those who are lonely or in need, people who cannot cope by themselves. When they cry out, not only for food and material goods, but for love and recognition, their openness, their eyes, their flesh, their whole being, seem to call forth what is most beautiful in those who accept them and who enter into relationship with them: compassion, respect and tenderness. We may admire someone who is strong – but the weak awaken our hearts. Their cry can, of course, also have the opposite effect: people close up and refuse to hear their cry of loneliness.

Is this not why the Word became flesh? Is this not why he emptied himself and became a little child in need, a humble, wounded person? God does not just want to be worshipped as a distant, wonderful, admirable God. God wants to reveal love: love that is communion, love that is personal, love that is a heart-to-heart relationship, love that is communication and friendship, love which implies a certain equality, love that is life and light. Is this not the very nature of God? God is three persons in love with each other, equal to each other in every way, giving themselves to one another in love and in communion, resting in one another. God is ecstasy and glory in love.

So the Word became flesh to tell us not to be afraid, but to lower our barriers and defence mechanisms, and open the doors of our hearts to let the Trinity of love share their ecstasy of love with us.

In L'Arche and Faith and Light, people with mental handicaps teach us how fragility, weakness, tenderness and communion are linked together. Weakness is not something bad, to be shunned. It can become a path to communion – or, rather, a place of communion. People with mental handicaps teach us not to be afraid of our own vulnerability. We too can become like little children, reborn in love. They teach us that the Almighty One is also the powerless one: Jesus is like a child or a beggar, inviting us, asking us, begging us, to open our hearts to let him in, so that he may reveal his glory in our fragile beings.

A source of unity

At the Last Supper, when Jesus removed his outer garments and started to wash his disciples' feet, he was breaking down the barriers that separated the powerful and the powerless, the master and the servants, the clever and the foolish. Through this scandalous gesture he calls us to unity in one body. Jesus is our peace. He has broken down the dividing wall of hostility that separates people from one another (Eph. 2:14).

L'Arche wants to share in Jesus' mission of breaking down the walls that separate people from one another. Living together, we want to build unity between the so-called capable and powerful and the so-called incapable, powerless. We are all human beings. Each one of us is important and unique; each has a gift to give to the body of the community and of the Church; each is loved by Jesus just as he or she is.

The more I live with people with mental handicaps, and the more I visit L'Arche and Faith and Light communities around the world, the more I discover how people are walled off from one another, frightened of one another. These walls, however, also protect people from their own inner chaos, violence, fears and the anguish of death, giving them a sense of being better than others. Surely the future of humanity lies less in competition, where there are winners and losers, and which often leads to war, and more in lowering the walls in order to discover the beauty of each person, and to live in communion and co-operation.

This mission of L'Arche becomes particularly evident in our inter-denominational and inter-religious communities, where we live together as Christians of different denominations, or as Hindus, Christians and Muslims. It is not always easy, but we are discovering our common humanity. We are not trying to create a new Church or a new religion. We want to respect the differences and help each one to be integrated into his or her own Church, place of worship, or religious tradition. We want to help each one discover that the essentials are to be open to God – to God's laws, to God's love – and to be open to each other, caring for one another. This is the challenge of our living with weak and fragile people, who in their littleness and trust are calling forth our hearts to love.

Pain and growth

In L'Arche, most people with handicaps find their place quite quickly. They discover their potential and grow to maturity. They find a certain inner peace. Some, of course, remain disturbed; they carry pain and anguish inside them. Not only do they carry the pain of their difficulties to communicate, to walk and to do things, but also the pain of humiliation and of rejection, the pain of having been seen for such a long time as having no value.

We often sing, 'The Lord hears the cry of the poor' – but we human beings do not want to hear this cry; the poor awaken our hearts and lead us on to the road of compassion, but they also disturb us.

L'Arche can only exist if men and women hear the call of God and the cry of those who have mental handicaps; if they discover their gifts and put down roots together in a simple community life, filled with ordinariness and mundanity, with pain, forgiveness and celebration. The long haul is not easy. Many assistants come to us for an experience of community. Often they are renewed and transformed by the experience: they discover faith and a new world where weakness finds meaning. But most are unable to stay because of other pressures. They need to find their own personal success in order to find themselves. Our daily way of life seems too simple, too monotonous.

A psychiatrist told leaders of L'Arche: 'You must understand that people with handicaps are not poor in L'Arche; they have found a home and peace of heart. It is frequently the assistants in L'Arche, especially the younger ones, who are poor and in need.' Many come from broken homes; they have had little spiritual and human formation before coming to L'Arche and are in a world that appears insecure.

Our challenge in L'Arche today is to learn how to help assistants grow in maturity, put down roots in community, find a peaceful rhythm of life, discover love and live this spirituality where they not only reveal love to the poor but where they allow the poor to reveal love to them.

Our life and our vocation in L'Arche is in some ways contemplative. We are called to be present to people enfolded in weakness. They touch and awaken our hearts. They call us to a simple lifestyle. They reveal to us Jesus, meek and humble of heart. But we are in a world that puts a high value on success and productivity. For 28 years Jesus lived a hidden, simple life in Nazareth. He lived the 'dailiness' of life with Mary, Joseph and their neighbours. We too must discover the beauty of this dailiness and ordinariness, through prayerfulness and through the beauty and the difficulties of community life, with all its celebrations and sharing, with all its relationships of love and of caring.

We see that assistants do stay when they discover L'Arche as a vocation, a place where they feel at home, a place where they can continue the journey to maturity, wholeness and holiness. In order to do this, however, they need to meet regularly with experienced guides who help them to find meaning in all the dailiness and pain, and to become more responsible for their lives; to help them find a pathway through pain and confusion, to live the cross and discover the resurrection. The message of L'Arche, like the gospel message, is beautiful. At first sight L'Arche may look like an ideal place, a place of the kingdom. But we must remember that it is founded on pain – it is for people in pain. It is not surprising, then, that there is pain in our communities. However, joy flows not from flight from pain, but from appropriating pain and letting it be transformed through love and grace.

L'Arche is rooted in the Church; we are a part of the Church. We can only live and grow if we are accepted and loved by the larger body of the Church, and not just seen as a good work for people with handicaps. We need to be discovered as a place of love which can become a source of life in and for the larger body of the Church. For this we need the help of theologians, pastors and spiritual guides, men and women of prayer, who give us support through their wisdom and love.

2

TOUCHING THE DEPTHS – RELATIONSHIP WITH THE POOR

GILLES LE CARDINAL

Gilles Le Cardinal reports from a communication workshop with L'Arche assistants. Their stories about handling difficult behavioural situations raise significant issues about relationships and communication. In particular, the need for consistency is illustrated. Confrontation builds, rather than undermines, trust, and so reveals the identity of both the wounded person and the assistant. When Jesus confronted Thomas the doubter, something similar happened.

This workshop was run at the request of a group of theologians, gathered in Trosly-Breuil by Jean Vanier to reflect on the way in which the poor may help us to reconstruct a Christian theology by becoming a source of unity. Assistants in the L'Arche community have profound experiences while entering into deep relationships with the handicapped people in their home. We suggested to a small group of assistants, who were involved in two years of philosophical, social and psychological studies in the context of the L'Arche *Ecole de Vie* (School of Life), that they should relate an event which was a profound experience for each of them. The experiences related below were written by seven assistants without collaboration. These experiences are set in the context of the personal development of individuals with different family backgrounds, education and cultural origins.

Thereafter we will attempt to highlight the common structural points of these experiences of daily relationships with mentally handicapped people. We will show that these relationships seem to go through a stage of decisive testing.

The seven stories

1. *Helping Virginie to explore the boundaries*

'One of my first important encounters with Virginie concerned the guidelines that we'd fixed to deal with her tendency to get herself invited to the other homes. Virginie had not lived at L'Arche very long; she was very young and rather pretty. She had been invited several times into one of the men's homes, where, it turned out, she didn't feel very comfortable. She would come home confused and upset. In addition to this, she would forget to warn her own home about her absences, and they would worry about her each time. So we made a rule that she wouldn't accept an invitation without the permission of her house-leader, and that she would not eat alone in the men's *foyers*. She agreed to this rule, and admitted that she was afraid when alone with the men who had invited her. As the person in overall charge of her *foyer*, I told her that if the situation recurred I would intervene.

'Two days later, I received the inevitable telephone call. The house-leader informed me that Virginie had not come home. I therefore called the men's home – and they confirmed that Virginie was indeed there. I told them that I would come right away to fetch her. When I arrived, they explained that Virginie had refused to leave when, already at table, she was told that she could not stay to eat. I was terribly tempted just to forget about the whole thing – but I was sure that if I did, it would be just the beginning of my troubles. I went into the dining room and I asked Virginie to leave the room, while reminding her of the reason for this. She told me that she wouldn't leave.

'I then offered her a choice between leaving willingly, or leaving by force – for, one way or another, she must leave. She refused to move, so I took hold of her with 20 people looking on, and I carried her screaming out of the room. We then went back to her home.

'From that moment on, Virginie and I were involved in a positive relationship. She was sure that I would always do what I said I would do. I've never again had to use force with her. I think that, through this baptism of fire, she tested my ability to be truly there for her when she needed me. Of course, I've had many difficult moments with her since then – but I think that a trust was established between us that has remained intact ever since.'

2. Getting Jacques out of his chair

'Jacques had lived with his parents until he was 32 years old, and worked in an occupational workshop during the day. When he came to L'Arche, Jacques never said "I", but rather "Jacques". He needed several weeks to locate his bedroom, the toilet, the coat rack, and so on.

'Like all people with Down's syndrome, Jacques needs reference points, and he very quickly claimed for his own a place on the living-room sofa. He resented it when someone took "his" place. In general, Jacques ate with pleasure, appreciating the pleasant surroundings of meals in the home. Very often, when the assistants invited everyone to come to table by shouting, "Dinner's ready", Jacques either didn't hear, or didn't want to hear. Even if an assistant made the effort to call him individually – "Jacques, time to eat" – he didn't budge. This kind of attitude irritated everyone. However, I noticed that in order to make him come to table more easily, you had to say almost nothing; rather, you had simply to come up to him and put your hand on his shoulder, inviting him gently to make the movement to stand up and take a few steps. That's all that was needed for him to come to table with the others, with a smile on his face.

'Jacques' attitude could have provoked a multitude of conflicts in the home. Complicated interpretations of his behaviour could have been built up. The house assistants could have argued about the pedagogical principles of various strategies which would have been complicated to put into practice. My discovery was made quite simply with my heart and my body. It was the gesture that Jacques was expecting, without explicitly being able to ask for it. It was the type of attention and personalised, concrete relationship which he needed – and which I needed in order to create a different relationship with him.'

3. Making an exception for Jean

'Jean openly disputed the house rule that everyone must be present at meals. He was frequently absent, and would miss the meal. In the end this created a serious problem in the home, which had to be dealt with through negotiation. Jean agreed to take part in meals most of the time, but asked that we be able to make exceptions. Although this touched the very heart of life in a L'Arche home, we organised a discussion of Jean's request.

'Faced with his insistence, we suggested making a new rule: "Those who wish may take an individual tray and eat alone once a week". Since then Jean waits impatiently for his tray-evening, but he never misses a common meal.'

4. Allowing Fanny to correct herself

'Meals are also a problem for Fanny. She chooses this time to be either aggressive or defensive. She looks for reciprocal relationships, and doesn't like authority, although she really needs it.

'Sometimes she gets upset at table: one Friday evening she suddenly became unbearably violent during dinner. I forced her to go up to her room, but that didn't stop her violence. She beat her head against the walls. I had to struggle with her to keep her from hurting herself. Eventually she calmed down, but she kept her distance all weekend, and didn't come back to eat with the others.

'On Monday morning I organised a meeting with her – but how to begin to talk about what had happened?

' "What were you trying to tell us on Friday at dinner? You upset everyone else because we weren't able to understand your behaviour."

'The weekend had given her time to reflect. "What I did wasn't a good thing," she said.

'She was the one who recalled the rules. As the authority figure, all I had to do was to welcome her into my arms. Both of us were in tears. It was the first time that she had ever said sorry. She was able to say that she wouldn't do it again.

'I had stopped her in her violence, and kept her from hurting herself at the risk of hurting myself. Then I waited all weekend. And on Monday, all I had to do was to let her express herself. The cause of her scene was trivial – a bad day in the workshop, for which the house wasn't responsible. But the discovery, the novelty, of the meeting on Monday, was that for the first time Fanny put into words the fact that violence during meals was forbidden. This came from her. She was aware that this rule was necessary for the life of the home.'

5. *Letting Jeanne touch my heart*

'As a baby Jeanne had been abandoned at the psychiatric hospital by her parents. She needed an enormous amount of attention. She consciously tested the assistants.

'One day, she offered pre-dinner drinks to everyone in the home, and took advantage of the situation to get drunk. As soon as I noticed the state she was in, I took her to the bathroom. She looked into the mirror crying: "Why doesn't anybody love me? I didn't ask to come into the world!"

'I answered her: "I love you, Jeanne". It was sincere.

'Jeanne went into her bedroom and vomited. Personally, I am horrified by such things, and I don't see myself as someone who is very understanding or sensitive – but I was deeply touched. I took the mop and I cleaned up without any feeling of disgust. She elicited from me all the tenderness of which I thought I was incapable. During the following evening, Jeanne was agitated, violent – she even broke her glasses. I took her into my arms and I repeated: "I love you, Jeanne!" I brought her a cup of tea and she calmed down. There was no need to call the house-leader, or to send her to the hospital (as we had imagined at one point).'

6. *Protecting Georges from his own violence*

'Georges is an anguished man who lives in his wheelchair. He is very finicky and finds it difficult to change his reference-points. During the holidays, his group was less strict with him than we are in his home for the rest of the year. On his return, this created some difficulties, and a feeling of general discomfort. How to reinstate the requirements that had been forgotten during the summer? I was a bit worried at the thought of my role as the authority figure, knowing that this would not be easy with Georges.

'On the first day back, I heard Georges yelling at an assistant in the kitchen. I stepped in immediately, violently grabbing Georges' wheelchair and replying in a tone louder than his. To my great surprise, he calmed down, and I understood how much the exercise of authority reassured him.

'I was relieved by this clash which happened so quickly, as it allowed me to assert my authority right away. In spite of that, before intervening I had felt ill at ease, because everyone was there, watching me and judging me. I felt that I had to be stronger than he. He was afraid of me because I yelled louder than he did. But after that incident, everything became easier. My forceful intervention helped him get his feet back on the ground. A bit later we were able to talk about his attitude: he admitted that he hadn't been fair. I asked his forgiveness for having reacted so strongly, and I explained to him that as house-leader I would not let him terrorise the others.'

7. *Accepting Armand's anger*
'Armand is a very anguished man, but he is also a very good worker who knows how to work well and hard. He had been working in a supermarket for the past three years, and he was proud of this. He had been living in a home which was close by. He then asked to move into an apartment, so we introduced him to Roger and Daniel, whom he already knew slightly, and he agreed to found a new, more independent home with them, of which I was named house-leader.

'Two weeks later, we learned that Armand had been fired a week earlier by a new manager at the supermarket, with whom he'd had a rather violent discussion. Armand had said nothing. I consulted the team in charge of the apartments, and it was decided that I should go and see Armand to tell him that we knew the truth, and that the following day he must report to the community workshop director in order to get a job there, as there was no possibility of finding work elsewhere. The team had warned me that this encounter would probably be violent, and that I should undertake it only if I wasn't afraid of Armand, and of the possibility of his being violent.

Wishing to live up to my new responsibility, I decided to go – my body mass should shelter me from the worst, as Armand is small.

'I met him, and delivered my message clearly. He ran straight to his bedroom and then came downstairs, yelling and screaming; he threw the metal cash-box containing the house finances at my face. Notes and coins flew across the room, and then he threw himself on me. I succeeded in grabbing his fists in mid-air before he could grab me by the neck, and we stood there holding each other for several very long seconds. Our arms shook with the effort, but he didn't manage to get his hands on me. After a time – which seemed like an eternity, but was really just a few seconds – he relaxed his muscles, laid his head on my shoulders and broke down weeping. I slowly put my arms around him, and then rocked him for a long time. He then told me everything. This scene was the starting-point of a long and tumultuous friendship based on trust in the face of every hardship.'

Pattern and significance in the stories

Virginie, Jacques, Jean, Fanny, Jeanne, Georges, Armand: so many individual scenes which lay the foundations for a discovery, a particular relationship, a chosen path, a certain trust.

In each case, conflict develops. In each case, the assistants are faced with the challenge of whether they have the courage to intervene, to do what they said they would, in the face of complete uncertainty, and the fear of what exactly might happen.

Each time there is the feeling of having to pass a test in the eyes of the person needing help: 'Will they do what they say, or will they be afraid of exercising their authority?'

Most often they have to act with the other assistants looking on. They, too, won't miss the chance to pass judgements. The psychological fear of being criticised for what they've done is added to the physical fear of the situation.

They do not know how the person will react. They sense that they are going to have to engage physically, more or less violently – from the simple gesture combining firmness and gentleness with Jean, to the frontal assault with Virginie, Fanny and Armand. Very often they are new to the responsibility, and fear that they have got off to a bad start.

The crucial situations almost always involve an established rule and a transgression of this rule. It is not surprising that meal-times, which have a fundamental importance in L'Arche values, are critical moments. Everyone knows that a transgression of this sensitive point will not go by unnoticed.

We might say that the handicapped person wants simultaneously to test two things: the rule itself, and the person who is responsible for enforcing the rule. The real test is of the solidity of these two things together.

Even if the assistants work as a team, at this moment the individual finds themself face to face, person to person. They don't really have time to think; they react instantaneously, with their heart and with their body. They learn about themselves at the same time as revealing themselves to the other person.

Circumstances cause them to feel some doubt at the beginning of the episode – but then they go ahead. They do what they feel must be done.

If they had to use force, they feel awkward, they discover their strength, they feel a bit afraid, just as they are afraid of the other person's strength. They don't know how it is all going to end. However, they discover that in fact it is not a simple question of strength. After a certain point, the person lets the assistant have their way, even if on a strictly physical level he or she could have won – especially when a female assistant comes face to face with a strong, robust man. The important thing is that the strength which is used does not spring from a desire to hurt the other person, but rather a need to control their violence. The assistant cannot leave the other person to their violence without reacting – for they need to feel protected from their own violence. They must not feel that their violence generates fear – that would simply amplify the violence. On the contrary, the violence runs up against a determination backed up by a rule – of which the person must be reminded, either on the spot or later, when together they go back over what happened.

It is necessary to put into words what the assistant and the wounded person went through together – first, by letting the wounded person express himself or herself; then, by reminding the person of the rule, and even sometimes by agreeing to modify this rule slightly – if possible, useful and necessary.

The person made a scene in order to be recognised as different from the others. This makes them an individual. The scene is a cry for others to take a personal interest in them, to spend time with them, to do things with them individually, and not as with the others. This search for individuality can produce an exception to the rule – in order, in fact, better to adhere to the rule. Some people simply need to be called by their name, and curiously this is sometimes sufficient to stop the violence. For others it might be a gesture, a touch, which they need to feel recognised, loved.

This interaction is important for the person, who is thus reassured and reintroduced into the group – but it is also a profound experience for the assistant. Assistants themselves are not always very comfortable with rules. They ask: 'Is it worth my taking the risk to enforce the rule? Do I trust myself enough to guarantee the enforcement of this rule?'

When they realise that holding fast to the rule calms down the person who is troubled, that this is the basis of a mutual and lasting trust, when they discover the ability in themselves to be a parent-figure by both enforcing the rule and welcoming the disobedient person (as the prodigal son was welcomed) – this is when they make an essential passage into adulthood.

It is this interaction which helps to make them a whole person, which reveals themselves to themselves, which builds up such a truly helping relationship that we no longer know who helped whom. It also reveals the identity of the person with a handicap, who asks to be recognised as unique – just as it reveals the identity of the assistants, who must dig deep down within themselves to find the strength to intervene. The cry of those with handicaps, expressed not in words but through conflict, calls forth from the assistants the response of which they did not know they were capable, and builds up their character by creating a trusting relationship.

Discovering true identity

These seven stories describe a true exchange which comes from deep within the two people involved, bringing to mind the relationship between Thomas and Jesus. Before his passion, Thomas said to Jesus: ' "Lord, we do not know where you are going. How can we know the way?" Jesus said to him: "I am the way, and the truth, and the life" ' (John 14:5).

This way becomes explicit a few hours later: it is the way of the cross, the ultimate violence done to Jesus' body in the name of the law. Thomas, deeply upset by this death, cannot believe in the resurrection which is the continuation of this way, and which the other apostles announce to him. This attitude excludes him from the communion of the group of apostles who saw the risen Jesus.

Jesus thus speaks personally to Thomas a week later. He says to Thomas: ' "Put your finger here and see my hands. Reach out your hand and put it into my side. Do not doubt but believe" ' (John 20:27).

This contact with the healing wound helps Thomas to relate to Jesus at the very heart of his identity as son of God, who died nailed to the cross and who is risen. Through this contact, Thomas draws a radical trust, and in touching the transformed wound of the risen Jesus, he simultaneously discovers both his identity as an apostle of the faith, and his failures. It is this contact, at once physical and symbolic, which establishes a new relationship, revealing the true identity of Jesus and of Thomas.

In the same way, the assistants, through the events which they chose to describe, discover the uniqueness of a person by responding to the call which comes from their very handicap. At the same time the assistants discover their own true identity, and a meaning of their life in the midst of the outpouring of trust which transforms this relationship and makes it fruitful.

'May a saviour come into my life,' said Jacques de Bourbon Busset. 'That is, someone who needs me.'

3

'DO YOU LOVE ME?' – STAYING SINGLE FOR THE KINGDOM

GILBERT ADAM

Gilbert Adam, through examples and testimonies, and by interweaving L'Arche experiences with Gospel narratives, develops a picture of the vocation, commitment and spirituality of those who share in the life of the community.

Incarnation and brokenness

L'Arche communities welcome people with a mental handicap, people who may have been left to feel poor and rejected; the communities fully recognise their dignity and vocation. Families, celibates, religious, priests, professionals – we form a great family unified by the face of the poor. Opening up to the poor offers to each, whatever their lifestyle, a specific gift for the Christian life:

> It's by being close to them that I have come to know men and women with a handicap better. 'Men and women': this rather vague and distant term which we use all the time doesn't seem to correspond with what we live in L'Arche! And yet, by being near to them, this term has taken on its full meaning for me, for I really encounter and accompany man and woman as God sees them, whether in first meeting them (simplicity, truth, love) or in their final embrace (agony, suffering and death). This phrase, 'men and women', makes me understand all the hidden greatness, the fullness and achievement of each person, as though they were meant to live a mystery, bringing together at the same time the joyful, sorrowful and glorious mysteries.

Mysteriously they have trodden the same path as Jesus from Bethlehem to Calvary. And now, like Jesus, they are a eucharistic Host; they are therefore vulnerable as the Host is. Their mysterious path is such that they have had to undergo everything, yet in doing so receive every good. They haven't, like us, cleverly avoided the cross or stepped around the shadows. They go before us. And we're a bit like the priest carrying the Blessed Sacrament: the tiny Host is ahead, it is everything – but we're the ones who carry it.

Jesus' body is vulnerable in this Host: it can perish; it can be profaned. The 'men and women' also possess this vulnerability. To ensure that no harm comes to this Host is to be attentive to this Mass. A book has recently been published entitled *The Shadow Obeys the Sun* – an expression I like very much. How true it is! How faithful is the shadow in following the sun at every moment. The shadow exists only because the sun exists; when the sun sets, it disappears.

The 'men and women' are like this faithful shadow, the sun's witness amidst all the mistiness – a deep shadow, not our half-lights. They make me understand how I come from God, what my shadows and present infidelities are, and how love traces the path.

If I want to be with them and accompany them, I have to share their grace with all of my understanding – to live from their mystery – this is where they lead me. They too are like this presence of Jesus in the Host, so efficacious, so silent.

And so the Christian communities of L'Arche become a caring environment for people in search of a meaning for their life. By coming to L'Arche, an assistant makes a decision which brings about a real change of view. The incarnation, the coming of the Lord Jesus, Son of Mary, in the flesh, will inevitably be offered to the assistant.

L'Arche offers such a varied and colourful world that I can experience the concrete love which is incarnated in the ambiguity of everyday life. After the first flood of light, when the warm, bright atmosphere of community life makes everything seem lovely, the shadows appear, and we see the truer face of each person with their traces of anguish, struggles and searching. Life with people who have handicaps will only go on emphasising the weight of differences, showing the other person as another.

Thus I am given the opportunity to be more responsible for my life, maybe to rediscover the faith of my baptism and to grasp better God's call to me. A commitment to L'Arche is lived within the context of the covenant: together those who would help and those with a handicap walk with the disciples of Emmaus alongside the risen Lord. Within this life with mentally handicapped people in L'Arche, remaining single for the kingdom may seem a possibility for me.

The uniqueness of each person

It is quite surprising to hear men and women at L'Arche talk about their choosing to remain single for the kingdom of God. A few had heard this call even before coming to L'Arche, and had responded to it within a different context. For some, it was when they arrived at L'Arche that they immediately felt a call to form a deep, close relationship with Jesus in person. For most, the gift of God was revealed to them through the presence or crying out of the handicapped person – and it is the ecclesial face of the community which has helped them to be open to this call. From the very beginning of L'Arche, we wanted to live with the poor, and this destiny binds us not only in everyday life, but also in the decisive choices of our personal lives.

Young assistants arriving at L'Arche, no matter what stage they may have reached in their own inner journey, can experience a true communion which involves loving people with mental handicaps for nothing other than who they are. This love – a love which unites all forms of true human love – is at its purest in the welcome offered to the handicapped person. A mentally handicapped person is capable of loving and being loved, and when we consider just how poor they are, how needy and deprived, we could say that this constitutes their very being. The only true way to love a handicapped person is in and with the very love of God.

For people who suffer from a mental handicap are generally unable to marry, and never know the joys of motherhood or fatherhood. They are more or less bereft of language, and of the cultural riches which nurture human friendships. Their family history having necessarily been painful, the heartbreaks they may have known before arriving in the community have, more often than not, damaged or confused for them the usual indicators of love. Their physical appearance, often at odds with their true age, is just one of the factors which deprives them of a clear place in family structures, in the order of loving relationships, in the social organisation of life's various stages. Before we attempt to restore for them, as far as we can, the usual conditions of a 'normal' life, we need to meet them where they are, in the nakedness of their painful existence, in the mystery that is their own, and in their vocation as loving and beloved people.

Those who are poor in their very being are made for that communion for which they yearn. As a new-born baby in all its vulnerability naturally evokes a loving response from its father and mother, so love may be stimulated in the heart of an assistant who lives, day in, day out, with a human being commended to his or her care by God. By attempting to respond to each person, we are led to a direct discovery of the mystery of every individual, and of each particular loving relationship in the light of God's love. Thus life in L'Arche communities may itself reveal a particular love and hope, which already exists as an implicit faith in God and in the mystery of each human person.

Claire's story

Claire was 30 when she arrived at L'Arche from a psychiatric hospital, where she had lived for six years after the death of her mother. She had spent all her childhood on a barge with her mother, stepfather and brother – barge people. Claire often referred to the hard life she had endured with her family: this – as well as her handicap – had affected her. Her constant need for attention, along with her aggressive behaviour, showed how much she had suffered. With equal intensity, Claire was also compassionate, a pleasure to others and a trustworthy friend.

Claire needed to be understood by brothers and sisters who, by a life of faith, could enter into direct communion with her suffering heart. In order to find inner peace, Claire needed to be bathed by this new love given by Jesus. Today we can say that Jesus has become a reality for Claire: she no longer puts him in the category of people she came across on her barge. Mary, the mother of Jesus, has also become important in her life.

Claire is gradually moving towards an acceptance of her status as a single woman – though there are still some problems to be dealt with. There are still times when Claire screams that L'Arche is curtailing her freedom, that her mother would get hold of a man for her whenever she wanted, that she never used to be 'locked up' as she is at L'Arche. And yet Claire has experienced a deep, spiritual awakening which enables her to cope with these crises, to go beyond the struggles and darkness. Claire can now distinguish between what brings her deep joy and peace, and what is superficial and a source of trouble to her, which won't lead to lasting happiness. We are on our way together.

Claire's discovery of the mystery of the presence of Jesus grew from the relationships that she lived with people anchored in their Christian faith. It is because we welcome Jesus in faith that he can reveal himself to us in our lives. And those things which are revealed to the mentally handicapped person can also be revealed to the young assistant searching for their path in life.

The community enables Claire to live and trust in this new love which is a Person, the Holy Spirit, the Father of the poor. The person seeking God can likewise live this experience of trust even before putting it into words, thanks to life in community. The community teaches us a new way of being with our brothers and sisters, for we are all children of our heavenly Father and are in his tender, loving care. Last but not least, in the face of the poor, the community reveals to us the face of Christ.

Solidarity in singleness

Life in L'Arche is an instant introduction into a universal communion with each person called to be saved, in so far as it is shared with the poorest person, and therefore with human beings in their deepest vocation. This is why L'Arche is by nature ecumenical – open to all who seek God, justice, love, from any Christian confession, from other faiths or simply from the integrity of their heart. In this sense, L'Arche's mission goes alongside that of Jesus' Church, and reflects its universality. In return, L'Arche receives from Jesus' Church confirmation of its own deep identity – an openness to the universality of Christ's salvation.

The community is led to think even more about its mission due to the presence in L'Arche of men and women called to be single for the kingdom. How exactly does the gift of singleness enrich our solidarity with those whose lives are marked by a mental handicap, enriched as it is also (but in a different way) by the presence of families living within the sacrament of marriage?

To live the single life in the joy of the risen Christ is equally possible for those who, because of their handicap, have had no choice about living in the celibate state, for whom the marginalisation that comes from their handicap is emphasised by the necessity of living outside the family structure. Assistants living in L'Arche thus take on the condition of the poor and the suffering, and through their free choice shed light on its meaning. We are all drawn on by the example of Christ, whose itinerant and celibate life posed questions for his followers.

For the families of these young assistants who commit themselves to remaining single, this raises real questions – especially when they consider the suffering entailed in living in L'Arche. It would be simpler and much easier to understand if L'Arche were a religious order – or even more, a professional centre. But isn't the unusualness, and the social indetermination of such status, a way of sharing a little in the lot of so many marginal people who are living in our world, loved by Jesus Christ? Isn't it a good way of participating in the suffering of the excluded, the unloved, those for whom rejection is their daily bread?

Married people challenge single people not to hide behind a mask of self-centredness that could become a snare. But our world also needs to hear that there is another choice. Life as part of a couple is not the only means of finding happiness. In L'Arche it is families and single people together, along with those entrusted to us, who form a community in the joy of the risen Christ. Every horizon is illumined by Christ.

Life in L'Arche brings with it a permanent challenge: how, on the one hand, to find the right amount of solitude necessary for rest and prayer; and how, on the other hand, to respond to the demands of the community. The warmer and richer the life of the community, the deeper may be the loneliness within the hearts of those who have to live daily with their handicap. Singleness also brings loneliness – though chosen, not enforced. This is healthy enough, as all human relationships imply some loneliness. But loneliness can prove unbearable. The agony of Jesus in the Garden of Gethsemane is like a constant beam on our path.

At the same time, we live close together in our homes, men and women, as one single body, called to build up the community. This experience, and our understanding of it, needs to be enlightened and deepened all the time, particularly since it is one of the most important areas of our lives. We do have the means of meeting these challenges, by opening ourselves up to the hidden, inner dimension of L'Arche, and so going further into the mystery of poverty lived by people with handicaps. They encourage us to follow them on this path, to come to know the presence of God who is ever at the heart of each one, and who never ceases to kindle our desire for him.

Thus the community reveals its deeply eucharistic identity. The living bread we receive makes us desire Jesus; and thirst quenched by the new wine only serves to sharpen our thirst. The parched cry of Jesus from the cross rings true in the depths of our heart: 'I thirst'. And so, for the person who follows Jesus on the path of a single life, loneliness offers the chance to grow in a life of union not only with the poor, but also with the crucified and glorified Christ.

We know that our life will be largely misunderstood by the world. And yet all that goes with being single – social marginality, a specific rapport with the body, availability and autonomy, a particular solitude, hidden productivity – will find, in L'Arche, the necessary conditions for a harmonious integration of our whole being.

Singleness and relationships

Experience has shown the extent to which community celebrations in L'Arche – particularly religious celebrations, and notably the sacraments of the Catholic Church – can become bearers of the revelation of God's mystery and of the mystery of Jesus.

In community life, Jesus reveals himself in subtly different ways: in the sacraments, in the liturgy and para-liturgies ('unofficial' liturgical acts), in the person with a mental handicap, in the community church, in the Bible. But the Eucharist is the height of the experience whereby the presence of Jesus is made known through people with mental handicaps and through their assistants. For men and women in search of meaning for their lives, the presence of Christ sought secretly shines in the faces caught up in this mystery. So at L'Arche the gift of community life very often leads towards living as a committed Christian.

Living day in, day out with the poor can prove to be quite a trial for the assistant. At some point everyone is bound to discover their own limitations and weaknesses. They discover that they have handicaps too – but more hidden ones. Encountering the poor puts people in touch with the depths of their being: in turn, each of them becomes poor and needy. The discovery of this deep need for healing and peace deepens the desire of each person to enter into relationship with God, the Other. And so they each discover that they are capable of taking the path of the Beatitudes. It could be that the assistant is already living the Beatitudes, following in the steps of Jesus, for this way of living with the mentally handicapped person leads to a very personal encounter with Jesus himself, the poorest of the poor. By living with the poor, the assistant can be faithful to Jesus in a very explicit manner, through living out the gospel. This can be the beginning of a radical commitment: to follow Christ in the light and movement of the Holy Spirit.

It may also lead someone from another religious tradition to come into communion with a mentally handicapped person, and to become completely devoted to the values of human solidarity, compassion, and universal love which are implicit in this encounter, even though the Christian dimension is not explicit.

Community life is not the only aspect of L'Arche to nourish the commitment of those who choose single life for the kingdom. It is also nourished by the unique relationship which can be created with a particular handicapped person. Having intuitively heard the cry of love, an assistant can ascribe an incomparable meaning to this, and a unique response can be awakened. Many personal vocations among assistants, whether they be single or not, stem from a privileged relationship with a handicapped person who has touched them. The assistants have been led to a particular place in their own vocation.

Laurent's story

Laurent arrived at L'Arche at the age of 18, after having spent 15 years in a psychiatric hospital. He had a very profound handicap, mental and physical. His parents had suffered greatly: Laurent never walked or fed himself, and he lived in a state of extreme dependence. A silent little prophet, he died, and went to be with Jesus on Ash Wednesday, 1991.

Laurent, sitting sloppily in his wheelchair, his hands twisted together and head thrown back, had a beautiful face despite his haggard expression. He bore the image of the tortured Christ. The assistant taking care of Laurent couldn't help but wonder: Who *is* Laurent?

From time to time, Laurent's gaze took in what was going on around him. Eye-contact with Laurent never lasted very long, but if by chance I caught his eye, it was an unforgettable – though fleeting – moment.

Laurent called out for a constant presence close by him – but did he have the capacity to call someone forth to follow on his path of solitude?

He asked for nothing, but took in what was going on around him. Being close to Laurent, you can sense the same presence as in the chapel: someone is there, but hidden. How can you discover Laurent? How can you enter into relationship with him?

The only meaning to Laurent's life can be found by reading the good news proclaimed to the poor.

It can be quite surprising to hear the reflections of all those assistants who have taken friends such as Laurent to Mass. They are unanimous in saying that they experience the Mass in a new way, discovering a new intensity of Jesus' presence, and receiving a gift of compassion leading to a new depth of communion. Whether the assistants have been able to follow the celebration or not, they receive something of the presence of God's mystery on the altar, a presence received by being in deep and intimate communion with their handicapped friends.

They thus discover a new way of serving both Jesus and the mentally handicapped person, who are mysteriously one, present in our common life. This life takes on a new dimension, for God is truly present with us. Such a powerful experience can bring the assistants to offer themselves to Jesus in his Church – which becomes Laurent's Church and the Church of all those who, like him, participate so personally in the mystery of Jesus. There is a privileged way of ensuring a presence close to Laurent: in rather the same way as parents quite naturally 'consecrate' themselves to their child. Through their faithfulness and constant presence, they are able to go beyond what they had thought were their limits by drawing on the life within them. Is there not something here of a spiritual parenthood? By silently demanding a total presence, Laurent can evoke from his assistant the total gift of himself: 'Do I have value for you? Are you capable of renunciation so as to walk with me, of following the way of the hidden good news for the sake of the kingdom? If I do have this value for you, life is going to have a meaning and the words from the Gospel won't seem empty any more.'

Is there not here a call to remain single for the kingdom? This very real parental love reaches the other, the handicapped person, in the

heart of his or her life and brings out strengths in the assistants –
such as the self-giving, and generosity which they never dreamed
they had. Here again, a balance has to be found: the fact of living in
community no longer satisfies all the possibilities of the person's
deeper calling. Still, Laurent – and those like him – will have played
a part in bringing an assistant to birth into the life of Christ. The
assistants also have a part in the new birth of a humanity, fulfilled
and opened up.

Marie-Noelle's story

Marie-Noelle, who was 19, came to The Seed when the home
opened. Severely handicapped, she needed help for the tiniest movement. During her childhood she had been cared for in different
institutions, but had been able to stay near her family. She was very
much loved by her parents, brothers and twin-sister Claire, who was
affected by the same handicap. In June 1990, Marie-Noelle died
unexpectedly after having been admitted to hospital.

'Happy are those who are invited to the wedding-feast of the
Lamb!' Our life is a great mystery, whose fulfilment will only be
found in the heart of our heavenly Father. Marie-Noelle, through
dying, has gone there for ever. In the gentle breeze which bore her
life, she listened to the sound of a merciful love, and gave her answer.
In what way? That is God's secret, but we sensed that she did
answer. Her frail body contained such a wonderful heart which
wasn't the least bit handicapped. It would quiver in its contact with
God and with others. Today we are still discovering how many hearts
she touched, and to how many of us she gave life.

In our chapel Marie-Noelle often heard the call of the Church
sound out: 'Happy are we who are invited to the wedding-feast of
the Lamb!' How happy she was to have been able to participate so
often in the Eucharist! How well she knew how to bring her com-
panions into a communion with Jesus. Now she is able to bring them
to him even more.

So we can grasp Jesus' meaning when he says in the Gospel that
those who have given up everything for the kingdom will receive a
hundredfold in return . . . with persecutions. There are always trials

of obedience for those who follow Jesus on the path of remaining single for the kingdom. Dying to ourselves is never very pleasant, even when all is bright and the Holy Spirit shows us where the will of God lies. The path is generally dark, and our sensitivity is not naturally adapted to the dark night of the soul.

It is very well and good to live in the eternal love of the Holy Spirit – but it gives us a longing for heaven. The joy of being together, of community, won't ever remove the deadly loneliness felt by some. But after the storm comes the sunshine, and so it continues. This constant change from brightness to darkness can prove quite disconcerting. Mary's compassion and Jesus' life are present in the life of the mentally handicapped person in L'Arche, and the same mystery is played out in the life of the assistant who has chosen to remain single for the kingdom. After a time of brightness, there may come a time of darkness and doubt. The joyful sight of a beautiful sunset may be followed by a rude, disturbed awakening.

Christ, the 'poor one' present in the handicapped person, will gradually take possession of whoever offers themself to him. And so the path is one of identifying with the poor. This is a further step in the calling to remain single. Not only do the assistants have to live a life of consecration by sharing their lives with mentally handicapped people, but they will also have to allow themselves to be identified with the poor in their suffering. This is essential in order to be joined to Jesus, who is the only true 'poor one'.

Jesus' call to a single life in L'Arche is seen in the context of his resurrection. Being risen in Christ, we can move forward in the same mystery of death and resurrection that he knew, and in which he still lives today within the Body of his Church. We can allow this mystery to take possession of us, body and soul, through a deliberate renunciation of any other plan in life. Nourished by the Eucharist, we can draw on the strength we need so as to go with him on his journey to Gethsemane.

An assistant's story

'When I got to know L'Arche, I was undoubtedly a broken person without much hope left in life. What touched me first of all in L'Arche was the quality of the relationships, and how each person was respected. I came to discover a community life where I was welcomed despite my wounds. I also discovered a deep thirst within me, even though I couldn't yet put a name to it. I could sense that the life of L'Arche was, deep down, inspired by Jesus, and I came to rediscover the genuineness of the gospel message, just as I had felt it as a child. All this bothered me, called me onwards and drew me further.

'I stayed because this very simple day-to-day life centred around the home got a grip on me. I was living close to Bruno, Maurice and the others, and little by little they revealed to me the mystery of a presence that lay within their suffering, in their capacity for love. They led me to meet Jesus, to offer my own wounds to him. They have been instruments of my conversion.

'This growth has also been nourished by the presence of people whom Jesus placed on my path. They listened to me, guided my searching and drew me onwards. It was also nourished by the sense of belonging more fully to a spiritual family. On a wider scale, I also grew to love the Church.

'I gradually became aware of my desire for an inner life. My prayer became more fervent. I adopted a very basic type of prayer, stripped of all its complications – a prayer which was firmly rooted in our common life in L'Arche, and where I had often recognised the mystery of Jesus on the face and in the heart of the poor person.

'Later on, I was led to discover the grace which lies in the sacraments, where Jesus silently gives himself to us. I came to draw stength from them. I can say today that I have come to know the tender love of a God who is a forgiving Father.

'The seeds of faith, which were sown in my childhood and then buried, have found in L'Arche the soil in which to grow, leading me to an inner peace and harmony. This path of conversion hasn't been without struggle, resistance and the short-lived temptation to give up. The commitment must be renewed daily with an ever-increasing sense of surrender, for the temptations are strong and persuasive.

'My desire for conversion draws its strength from the conviction that Jesus led me to L'Arche. It is he who invites me to be faithful even in the more difficult moments, to enter into a covenant with those who are at the heart of the community, who are most wounded. These people have led me to a hope and to an inner peace which stems from God.

'I often thank God for having given me, in L'Arche, a place in which to grow, and for this path leading towards a deeper fulfilment of my heart and of my whole being.'

✿ 4 ✿

I CAN'T SAY 'JESUS', BUT I LOVE HIM

GERARD DAUCOURT

Gerard Daucourt tells stories of the people among whom he lived in the L'Arche community in Rome. He emphasises especially the significance of prayer and the sacraments for people with mental disability, and for those who accompany them. His account also brings out the special grace of God shown to those whom the world discounts.

Fabio's night – and Luciano's pain

We don't know why Fabio went out alone the other evening. It wasn't the first time that he'd been outside the house. He likes animals, and goes to see the neighbourhood dogs – or to look for his own, which had run away. That particular evening, Fabio had taken part in the celebratory meal to welcome Bernadette, the new person in charge of Olive Tree Hostel – but he had refused to do the drying-up and had disappeared. No one can know what was going through his mind; there are so many possible interpretations.

We don't know why Fabio left. We don't even know exactly where he went, or what he did, or what someone did with him. At 15 years old, Fabio doesn't talk, can't hear and can't write. He can make signs to ask for things, to express his agreement or disagreement, and to pray. When the priest arrives at the community, Fabio makes a sign of the cross (such as he can), which means: 'Will there be a Mass?' If there is, Fabio either shrugs his shoulders, to indicate: 'I don't want to go', or he touches his chest, meaning: 'I want to go – and I want to be the altar boy'. I love that freedom of Fabio's.

To try and understand what is really going on for Fabio – for example during a meeting – it is necessary to make gestures. He then replies with other gestures, with a smile or with a tensing of the face. So it's impossible to find out from him what happened during the night when he was missing. The police found him at 9 a.m., half-dressed, a long way from the community. It is inconceivable that he made such a long journey on his own. Some young people saw him in front of the church shortly after he went out. A police dog tracked him to the front of the church at 2 a.m., but the trail then disappeared. Fabio couldn't have asked his way, or taken himself anywhere. With his twisted hands he can't even thumb a lift. Two medical examinations have proved that he wasn't subjected to sexual violence. Non-violent contact, with careful respect to his human privacy, may have taken place. That also we will never know. Not knowing is difficult to accept.

Fabio would have been happy to get into a car: he trusts everyone, and always offers his friendship to everyone, silently. If someone had taken him with honourable intent, they would surely have left him at a hospital or police station. Did that bad person repent and give up on their bad intentions? So perhaps he was taken by an evil person who changed their mind when they discovered that Fabio is deaf and dumb. We know that horrible crimes are committed because their perpetrator was afraid of their victim talking – but Fabio will never talk. Paradoxically, maybe he owes his life today to his weakness.

During that night of worry, for him and for us, there were more than 20 of us going around all the roads, searching all the building-sites, questioning all the passers-by, visiting all the nooks and crannies – community assistants, the police force, neighbours and friends, all looking for a 15-year-old deaf and mute boy, with physical and mental disabilities.

Who would believe that we were looking for happiness, Fabio's and ours? The happiness of someone who is neither active in today's society, nor productive for the economy, nor sought-after for his future social success – but who was in danger of being lost. Fabio so often reveals to us our ability to forgive, our capacities for loving, for reconciliation, for the joys of community life, that a large part of our own happiness was in danger of disappearing. Through Fabio we are reminded of Jesus, the source and revelation of that happiness which is in everyone. Our friends, the Little Sisters of Jesus at Tre Fontane, took over in prayer, and in our chapel, from 2 a.m. onwards, the Blessed Sacrament was exposed and adored. By his absence, Fabio brought us all together and made our mutual love grow, as well as our faith – our love for him, and our love for the One who is present in the smallest.

I can't stop myself from thinking about the stranger whom he must have met, and I can't stop thinking about Luciano, a 30-year-old man who shared with me one day his deep secret and his suffering. He is sexually attracted by adolescents. Ten years ago, he was accused of having a relationship with a young boy: he went up to his room, ready to commit suicide. But at the last minute, his faith in God saved him. A friend led him to hope. He put himself in the hands of a psychiatrist. 'Now I understand myself much better, but I'm not cured; I still get those urges', he says. He has a terrible struggle, but so far, he is winning, and has never offended again. Who would believe that he told me, during one of our meetings: 'It's as if there were two Lucianos: one Luciano unable to control this powerful attraction towards adolescents; and another Luciano who keeps his rosary beads in his pocket and prays to the Virgin Mary to save him. "Go away", I shouted at a young man coming to my flat door.' Then he asked me: 'Pray for me and for those whom I meet, so that we may always be saved, even at the last minute'.

The loneliness and suffering experienced by Fabio and by Luciano are very different – and yet are strangely alike. Why was Fabio born like that? 'Why do I have these feelings?', Luciano asks. As there is no answer, it's all too easy to run away from Fabio and to condemn Luciano. These are the most spontaneous and common reactions.

Fabio calls out for love, ceaselessly, in the name of Christ who identifies with him. Who has ever been excluded from the love of Christ? Even if one day Luciano were to sin again, due to his uncontrollable urges, and if human justice had to follow its course and society had to protect itself – even so, only the merciful, divine Judge would know the depths of his heart; for whatever else he may be, Luciano will always remain one of God's children, needing to be loved and to love.

You, the stranger of the other evening who took and then abandoned Fabio: you let yourself be drawn towards light, instead of drawing him into darkness; and if you ever meet him again – or another like him – you will see that he is able to lead you on into the love which flows peacefully from the depths of the heart, and into the joys of life. You may still have some nights of loneliness, suffering or even horror – but Fabio would make some stars shine there.

Meeting Christ in prayer

We had travelled from Rome to Lourdes, and were staying in the Cité Saint-Pierre du Secours Catholique. It was raining and cold. In one room, we had set up a cross on a little mound of stones, and after singing a hymn, we were each invited to come and pray in front of the cross, in our own way: in words, through silence, by bringing up a flower, or whatever.

Big Giorgio, who can only say a few words, often suffers profound inner torment, which he expresses sometimes by an achingly sad expression, sometimes by ignoring some member of the community, or even, very occasionally, by violent outbursts. He came and knelt before the cross. After a long silence, he murmured three times: 'Jesus, heart . . . Jesus, heart . . . Jesus, heart' – making gestures as if leaving his heart at the foot of the cross. It was a Good Friday morning.

For another service in the hostel, we had enlarged a picture showing Mary carrying the infant Jesus in offering, with Jesus opening his arms and smiling. I had explained that we were asked, like Mary, to receive Jesus and to offer him to others; and that we should be like Jesus, smiling and with open arms, ready to welcome the whole world. Perhaps Paolo didn't really listen to my words, but he had taken note of the gestures: those of Mary and Jesus in the picture, and my gestures during the explanation. At the end of the meeting, it was suggested that we pray for a few moments. Immediately Paolo lifted his hands in offering, then smilingly opened his arms wide – and he made us copy these gestures several times. Mass for the whole community followed shortly afterwards – and Paolo carried the picture of Jesus and Mary, and was asked to teach the whole community how to pray. Pointing to the picture, he repeated the gestures several times until all the community members were imitating him. After that Mass, and often during other celebrations, I would say: 'Paolo, remind us of how we should imitate Jesus and Mary'. Paolo would then turn towards everyone and, wordlessly, invite us to the offering and the welcome.

For months, Maria lay on the floor or distracted herself with a book during evening prayer. But now she is often peaceful and still. In her own way, she traces the sign of the cross – for she is autistic, all shut up in her own world. Calming hymns and silence bring her peace. She likes the lighted candles in front of the altar and the statue of the Virgin, or in front of the Bible. When the time comes to blow out the candles, she takes one to Armando, who is lying still in an assistant's arms, and presents him with the candle for him to blow it out. She began to do this at about the same time as she was entrusted with the task of preparing the 'mixer' part of Armando's meal. No one ever had to explain to her that one can love by praying and serving.

Armando takes part in prayer by his presence and his silence. Sometimes he is more active, smiling or waving his arms around. One evening I carried him in and, throughout the community prayer, his eyes were fixed on the altar and the lighted candles. One of the assistants thanked the Lord that they had a priest at the heart of the community. At the words: 'Thank-you for the presence and the ministry of Father Gerard', Armando turned his head towards me with a big smile, then immediately turned back to the altar and the candles.

Father Luis, a young priest from Venezuela, was getting ready to return to his country after two years of study in Rome. I wanted him to know L'Arche, so he came to concelebrate with me. At the end of the Mass, Armando, carried by Guenda, the person in charge, brought him a little candle. 'Armando hopes that you have seen the light of Jesus shine here with the little ones. We hope that you will carry it in your heart, and that it will often shine during your ministry in Venezuela', said Guenda, putting Armando into Father Luis's arms, where he remained during the last hymn. Father Luis said to me afterwards: 'I tell you, I was very afraid of coming here because I'd never really met disabled people. Now I'm very happy.' After that, whenever I visited, I used to say to Armando, to whom I often entrusted my prayer-concerns: 'Don't forget to pray for Father Luis'. Each time, he answered with a smile. Then one day, he wrinkled his nose – for Armando, a negative sign. I hesitated for a moment on its meaning, then I asked him: 'Don't you want to pray for Father Luis any more?' He was still wrinkling his little nose, so I asked another question: 'Maybe I'm getting on your nerves by always asking you that. It's not worth saying it to you. Is that it?' A smile came. I'm sure I could translate it: 'Of course that's what I think. Trust me.'

There's so much that could be said about evening prayers in the hostels. They are so varied, and the Lord often talks to us through our disabled friends' simple gestures. They often use Jean Vanier's book, illustrated by nuns of the Little Sisters of Jesus. Sometimes Marie-Hélène shows painful pictures: and we pray with her that the Lord may give her peace of heart. But she, and many others, also find pictures of joy, of duty or of reconciliation – and they're often linked to one of the day's events.

Twice a year, we organise a two-day spiritual retreat. I remember the one when, to prepare us for our pilgrimage to Lourdes, we decided to introduce our friends to the rosary. It is difficult to recount what happened. We had meditated on the mystery of the life of Christ by praising his Mother, and by asking her to pray for us. Each one came up in procession to receive a rosary: 'Receive this rosary to pray, asking Mary to help you to know Jesus better so that you may follow him better'. Together, we said the rosary, saying only the first part of the Ave Maria and adding a clause to it: 'Hail Mary, full of grace, the Lord is with you, blessed are you among women and blessed is Jesus your child; Jesus is the friend of the small ones and the poor' – or even, ' . . . Jesus is present in all of us', or ' . . . Jesus who died and rose again to save humankind.' Each one was proud to have their own rosary. We attached it to Armando's arm. Vittorio had to make sure it was in his pocket every five minutes. We could see Paolo on his own, moving his lips as he said the prayers. Giorgio carried Lucia in his arms, and persevered in making her feel all the rosary, bead by bead. Fabio played with his, and every now and then paused to look at the cross. Marie-Hélène was thrilled, as she was able to say all the words of the Ave Maria.

An assistant said to Vittorio one day: 'When you're sad or you're angry, when you're suffering because you can't speak to express your resentments, go and kneel in front of the altar. Tell Jesus everything. He knows you and he understands you. He speaks to you in your heart.' Several times we surprised Vittorio, even during rest-times, kneeling alone in front of the altar in the small chapel. One day, he came to get me when I was preparing some books and magazines for a meeting. I understood that he wanted to show me something, but as I was in a hurry, and somewhat anxious about the meeting, I asked him to to come back later. He insisted. I refused more firmly; he insisted more firmly. Seeing that I wasn't going to co-operate, Vittorio grabbed me by the arm and made me follow him. He took me to the chapel, made me kneel down in front of the altar, and left – knowing, as I had failed to know, that this was exactly what I needed. A few minutes later, he came to fetch me to take me to a friend of the community who was passing through, and with whom I was to share a meal.

Meeting Christ in the Eucharist

At eight years old, with his serious disability, was Fabio ready for his first communion? One evening, after prayers, we invited him to kiss Jesus. On the altar of the small chapel is a statue of the child Jesus in a crib, opening his arms wide and smiling. Seeing Fabio approach the altar, we all assumed that he was going to embrace the statue – but he went straight to the aumbry, and kissed its door. He knew exactly where Jesus was truly to be found. From that day on, we began to prepare Fabio for his first communion.

A few years later, we were waiting for a similar sign to help us decide whether Armando was ready to receive the sacrament of the Eucharist. Should we be content with his smiles when we told him of Jesus' assurance that those who eat his body and drink his blood live in him and that Jesus lives in them (John 6:56), and that those who take part in the Eucharist become one body? Trusting in the Lord, who alone knows the true faith of those who receive his sacrament, we leaned on the belief that communion is primarily a divine gift granted to the poor – which we all are – and the decision was taken that Armando should have his first communion. The day came: the whole community, and about 30 friends, surrounded our little brother who, lying peacefully in Anne's arms, didn't stop smiling and opening his eloquent eyes. During the homily, I spoke first to Armando, telling him that Jesus' gift wasn't just for him, but was also to enable him mysteriously but honestly to reach out to many other people whom Jesus wanted to unite in his love. 'From this day forth, you will receive extra strength to enable you to experience true communion and unity. Jesus chose you, and gives you his grace, through the sacrament, to help us to meet him, to love him and to love one another.' Then addressing myself to the community, and especially to the friends, I explained how the Eucharist is food for the needy:

> In the person of Armando who, with his severe and visible disability, receives the sacrament of the Body of Christ, we are reminded that the poorer we are, the more Jesus wants to give himself to us. We all have disabilities – for example selfishness, a gross disability of the heart – but we are often able to hide them. Some people bear an enormous burden of suffering which they aren't able to share – perhaps stemming from emotional or sexual damage or abuse, from disabling relationships. Other people think that their problems are insurmountable, or their sins unforgiveable. Today, through Armando, Jesus says to us all, especially to the weakest and the poorest, to those who believe themselves to be rejected: 'I love you and am waiting for you'.

During the celebration meal which followed the Mass, five people –

four of whom hadn't received the sacrament for a very long time, and one who was seeking faith – came to talk to me; and, from that day onwards, they all began a spiritual journey with Christ. I still see them occasionally. We didn't have any dramatic signs beforehand to reassure us that Armando was ready to receive the Eucharist; but we had confirmation immediately afterwards: from the day of his first communion, Armando became more than ever a unifying agent for us, expressing the truth that Jesus died, 'to gather into one the dispersed children of God' (John 11:52), who live in him and are nourished by him.

Armando can only swallow a tiny morsel of the Bread of Life. We have a photo, which I love dearly, showing Pope John Paul II leaning carefully towards Armando, trying to find his little open mouth into which to put the Body of Christ. The great respect with which the pope carries the ciborium, and the concentrated look he is giving Armando, are for me signs of his faith in the presence of Jesus both in the Eucharist and in the poor people.

Whether Giorgio is participating in a Mass in the community's chapel or in a parish, he has a strong feeling of its being a moment of unity among those present. He understands that the source of that unity is Christ. When the priest prepares to distribute communion, Giorgio often stands up – even in parishes where he doesn't know anyone – turns to the congregation and, with gesticulations and with his very limited vocabulary, says: 'Come on ... everyone ... everyone ...!'

Sometimes Maria or Lucia would refuse communion – a freedom of choice which we respect. It's not easy to interpret their refusal – though on one occasion I felt that Lucia had refused the sacrament in order to remind me of her own dignity and need for attention. Usually, I bend down and carefully show her the sacred Host before offering it to her, saying: 'Lucia, Jesus' Body'. On that particular day, I wanted to give it to her straight away, without having first made eye-contact. By refusing to receive it, she reminded me of how I should always be aware, if only for a moment, of the relationship which links the person giving the Lord's Body with the one who receives it.

Each week, on Thursday afternoons, the exposition of the Blessed Sacrament takes place for an hour in the community chapel. Long periods of silent adoration are interspersed with short Bible readings, and the singing of peaceful hymns. All the members of the community come to pray there briefly, a few at a time, without anything being organised. Those who are independently mobile sometimes stay there for a long time.

For the night-long vigil from Maundy Thursday to Good Friday, one assistant and one disabled person put themselves down for half-an-hour. Last year, at 11 p.m., I was with Fabio. When our half-hour was up, Fabio signed to me that I could go, and he started praying again, his head lowered and his hands joined together as much as he could with his twisted fingers. He stayed in that position for another half-an-hour.

Our brothers and sisters with learning disabilities clearly enjoy praying in silence, as well as with hymn-singing, in which they join by clapping their hands or even making dancing gestures. In our community, we never sing the Sanctus without hand-clapping accompaniment: it's a joyous acclamation of the Lord whom it is 'meet and right to praise', as the preface says. Throughout the homily I refer to the community's life as much as possible, and I ask for assent (or disagreement!). Marie-Hélène and Maria, each in their own way, are able to say how they have understood the words of Jesus heard in relation to their own lives.

When it came to the intercessions, the assistants used to say a prayer in the name of the person who couldn't speak and whom they had accompanied to the Mass. But one day, Vittorio got up, and came to murmur some onomatopoeic sounds in my ear; then Giorgio began to say the names of assistants or friends or his family members. On another occasion, Paolo got up and turned towards the congregation, saying his usual syllables: 'Budo, na, ecco, uenda, Kesu'. I asked him if he wanted to request something from Jesus ('Kesu', for Paolo). He nodded, and so I invited him to turn to the altar in order to help him to differentiate this occasion from times when, during a celebration, he begins to address the assembled company, clowning around a bit, using a fork as a microphone, and seeking attention. Since that time, he often takes part in the intercessions, by staying peacefully in his seat and making lots of gesticulations so that 'Kesu' can really understand what he is saying. When he has finished, I conclude by saying: 'For all that Paolo has confided in you, Lord we pray you'.

Sometimes the intercessions are led in such a way that Armando, Silvia, Valentina, Lucia, Maria and Fabio understand that they too are invited to express a prayer: Marie-Hélène carries a small, lighted candle which she hands to each person in turn, to signify that it's their turn to speak to the Lord in everyone's name.

Fabio, who can't hear, can't talk and can't read, needs help to join in the Mass. This is what we do: just before the Gospel reading, I pick up the lectionary, along with Jean Vanier's book, illustrated by one of the Little Sisters of Jesus, opened at a picture which relates to the day's Gospel reading. Only after having said: 'The Lord be with you . . . The Gospel according to . . .', do I take the book to Fabio and do I begin the proclamation of the Gospel – at the same time as an assistant explains the picture to Fabio.

Receiving absolution

We had a day of penitence when each disabled person had to find, on their own or with the help of an assistant, a gesture, a sign, a drawing, a photo, a hymn, to try to express what they understood by the sacrament of absolution which they were each to receive. Vittorio appeared with a big boulder which he showed everyone, clasping it firmly to his heart. Then he gave it to the priest and went to embrace all the members of the community, laughing. The sin, the forgiveness through the priest's ministry and the reconciliation: all was remembered, all was symbolised.

Maria can hardly speak, and only murmurs 'Hi, hi' – her almost incoherent syllables of agreement – during confession. Often she's in a hurry to leave. What does she understand by it, I wondered? One day, she took me into the little room where I usually heard confession, pulled up two chairs, fetched a crucifix which she put on the table, and sat down. Very astonished, I immediately understood and said: 'Maria, do you have a suffering, a sin, something heavy in your heart, that you want to tell Jesus?' 'Hi! Hi!', was her reply. Slowly I gave her absolution, adding: 'All that I have said means that Jesus loves you, and wants you to be happy and help the others to be happy'. And Maria was saved.

Once, while I was getting ready to celebrate Mass, Giorgio came in and said: 'Mass ... Mass ... bad heart ... angry'. He made me understand that he was angry with an assistant. I assured him that during the Mass, Jesus would give him peace and that he should also pass on the peace of Jesus. Even before the start of the celebration, he went to hug the assistant with whom he'd had difficulties.

We are very insistent that all the community members understand that, among ourselves, we should actively demonstrate Jesus' forgiveness, as shown in the sacrament. When Paolo has done something silly, or refused to do a duty or he has behaved badly, he becomes very unhappy as soon as he has been reprimanded. He tries to sit next to the person who told him off, or he scans their faces to see if they're still angry or if perhaps they have forgiven him. He definitely wants a sign – and his joy overflows when he can shake hands, make peace and receive a kiss.

What was Armando thinking when, for several days, he refused to let Bernadette feed him? He firmly shut his mouth, and unusually accepted food from another assistant. Then Bernadette remembered that, when she'd been particularly busy, she had been rather brusque with him. Trying yet again to make him eat, and faced with his refusal, she said to him: 'If I hurt you the other day, I'm sorry'. Armando gave a big smile and opened his mouth wide.

Giorgio sometimes has violent fits, though we don't know what triggers them. During these, he shouts obscenities or insults, hides himself or hits himself, and even hits the others. One day, a fit came on at the start of a Mass. He went from one end of the chapel to the other, disturbing everyone; then he threw hymn-books at people's heads. An assistant tried quietly to calm him down – he began to bang his head violently against the wall. He was asked to leave, but he refused. Several assistants tried to take him out, but he fought back violently. When it was time for the sermon, I suggested (for the sake of the younger members) that the whole congregation go out and pray in the big room next door. Once Giorgio had left, we all returned to the chapel, where we began a long prayer asking for peace – for Giorgio and for us. The hymn, '*Ubi caritas et amor, Deus ibi est*', alternated with the intentions, then the Mass continued.

Giorgio soon returned, looking sad and serious, and leaned against the wall at the end of the chapel. Then he came forward and prostrated himself, kneeling at the foot of the altar in front of everyone – he didn't move from there. When the time came to exchange the peace, I asked him if he wanted to receive the sign of Jesus' peace. He accepted it, but didn't pass it on to anyone – which he usually does so joyfully. He also agreed to receive the communion, still remaining on his knees and prostrated. When it came to the last hymn, I was standing, as usual, in front of the small statue of the Mother of God who offers her Son. Giorgio got up and put his hand on my shoulder, and under cover of the singing, I murmured: 'Have you received the peace of Jesus?' He replied, 'Yes'. I told him that he should give it to the others – so straight after the Mass, he began to hug as many of us as he could – and by evening, he was reconciled to everyone and had found peace of heart again.

I am occasionally asked, 'Why do you hear Armando's or Lucia's confession?' Some people think that they can't understand the meaning of the confession, or that it's not really a confession when they don't speak, or even that Armando and Lucia are so small, so weak, so disabled, that they are incapable of committing sins. Yet Armando and Lucia are able to refuse food, capable of showing their bad moods, their impatience. To what degree are they responsible for their actions? Fortunately, I don't know. But they are extremely attentive when, during the confession, I say to them:

'Jesus who loves you gives you peace. He takes you completely into his love. If you've had times when you haven't loved him enough, or you haven't loved others enough, we lay them before him now. Then he repeats to you that he loves you, and that he'll continue to trust in you so that, for you, his love will shine. We say thank-you to Jesus who always loves us.'

Those who see confession primarily as a test of our faults, or even as an account of our progress or lapses in our life of faith, would maybe be surprised that Armando and Lucia make confessions, and that I speak to them in such a straightforward, or even simplistic, way. But each time I do it, I am myself taken to the heart of that extraordinary sacrament. God's forgiveness is a permanent reality into which we are invited to enter, which we must first welcome. I myself must make my confession as clearly as possible, according to all my abilities – but I should above all listen to Jesus, who sees me as a poor sinner, and repeats to me each time:

> 'Since you have come back to the one who has called you, know that I have restored you to the grace of your baptism, that I chose you and that I don't go back on my choice. I need you to be my witness. Recognise your sins as much as you can, but above all, give me your weakness so that I reveal my strength.'

And this is the same Jesus who, through Armando and Lucia, reminds me of the basics of this sacrament when, in his name, I hear their confession.

'Lord, bless us through the poor for whom you care'

The community liturgy of L'Arche contains this invocation: 'Lord, bless us through the poor for whom you care'. We can easily miss the true meaning of blessing: in the Bible, blessing is the gift of God. Jesus blessed the bread before multiplying it. Blessing also means giving thanks for God's gifts, as shown in one of Jesus' prayers: ' "I thank you, Father, Lord of heaven and earth, because you have hidden these things from the wise and the intelligent and have revealed them to infants" ' (Matt. 11:25).

God's great blessing to us – a blessing that contains all other blessings – is the gift of Christ himself. 'Blessed be the God and Father of our Lord Jesus Christ, who has blessed us in Christ with every spiritual blessing in the heavenly places', wrote Paul to the Ephesians (Eph. 1:3). The Eucharist, which contains Christ, thus contains all God's blessing for us. On earth, there are no blessings more perfect. Participating in Mass is being blessed by God, with everything he gives us in and through Jesus.

As the fullness of divine blessing is in Christ, all the signs, all the ways offered by the Church through which we meet Christ and receive his grace, are also forms of divine blessing. As the Church is the mystical Body of Christ, so to be a member is to participate in God's blessing. As Christ is himself the expression, the word of God, so to listen to, read, and meditate on holy Scripture is participating in God's blessing.

And as Christ is identified with the little people, the poor and the suffering, so to meet them, to listen to them, to be at their service, to share their lives, is participating in God's blessing. ' "Just as you did it to one of the least of these who are members of my family, you did it to me" ', said Jesus (see Matt. 25:31–46). It's he whom we meet in the poor and the suffering. So our work is not only about doing something for them, but about receiving something – or rather someone – from them: Christ himself, in whom all the fullness of the divine blessing is found. Through the poor and the little people, God blesses us in Christ.

Those who have received the grace of sharing the lives of the poor know that this blessing isn't just a pious thought or a subjective religious feeling – but rather is a profound reality. They know all that they receive from the poor, the little people, who ceaselessly appeal to what is best in human nature, who push us to let go of our selfishness and our pride, and who share with us riches of tenderness and joy.

L'Arche communities are privileged places where we can experience the Christian paradox: we are enriched by poverty. It is no good trying to explain it in words: it has to be lived. The assistants and those who regularly work with the poor and needy benefit from this grace. Friends and neighbours can benefit from it too – they say that each time they come into a community with an open heart, they receive more than they ever give.

The blessing of God at L'Arche means all this and more. And we ask for and receive that blessing every day: 'Lord, bless us through the poor for whom you care'.

At the Mass of the Virgin Mary's Immaculate Conception, on 8 December last year, I took Lucia in my arms so that she, with me, could give the final blessing. Lucia lifted up her little hand at the same time as me, and even if she didn't really make the sign of the cross (in fact she grabbed my glasses while the congregation was saying 'Amen'!), we were together a double sign of God who, in Christ, blesses us through priests and through the poor.

❧ 5 ❧

L'ARCHE: THE COMMUNITY AND ITS RELATIONSHIP TO SOCIETY

RONAN SHARKEY

A person with a foot in both worlds (living in a L'Arche community and working outside it), Ronan Sharkey seeks to explore the relationship of L'Arche to wider society. He approaches this as a political philosopher, and his discussion is conducted within that discourse. Democratic society as simply the sum of individuals fails to create purpose, and the pluralism of collectives generates fear. In modern economies, interpersonal relationships are subordinated to ownership. Communities like L'Arche cannot be expected to resolve all the problems of liberal individualism, but they can provide a context in which traditions and narratives give unity to a human life, and integrate suffering and death.

Why do people come to live in L'Arche communities? More intriguing still, why do they stay? Newly arrived assistants in the L'Arche community to which I and my family belong must often feel that they have entered a different world – or at least a different dimension of the world with which they are familiar. The 'world outside', the world of the wider society, seems to live in a virtually permanent state of crisis and confusion as to the moral and spiritual values it can collectively proclaim without compromising the freedoms of the individuals of whom it is composed; but although, from the perspective of society as a whole, the chief concern seems to be the protection of the individual's personal liberty, many of the individuals themselves feel confusedly that some sense of the meaning and orientation of their lives should emerge from the fact of living with others, living in society, not just from individual choice. In stark contrast, the life of the community visibly enriches, strengthens and gives direction to the lives of those privileged to share it. The result is not unfrequently that even short-stay visitors feel their lives have taken a different direction, thanks perhaps to a deepened understanding of what it is to be a human being, as a result of being here.

This essay is in part an attempt to answer the question of what exactly in L'Arche gives it this particular quality. I want to approach it by looking at the related question of the contrast that establishes community as having an identity distinct from, and in important respects opposed to, the wider society. In this process, some elements of an answer to the first question will emerge – but the issues of identity and contrast have implications for any Christian community – though as will become clear, the term 'community' needs to be used with some care. Indeed, in the case of L'Arche there is in one respect a resemblance to society as a whole, for both are strikingly paradoxical: take, as an example, the contradiction between the socially corrosive ideology of economic efficiency and the wastefulness of the economies that proclaim it. To this world, L'Arche presents another and very different kind of paradox, no doubt accentuated in the case of the community in Trosly by the charm of the peaceful, cloistered, rural setting: it is an upside-down world, a world where the poorest and weakest have the places of honour; a world which, though it accepts the need to balance its budget and encourage its members to assume responsibilities with efficiency and competence, is radically opposed to inequalities of status and wealth, to violence, fear and isolation, and above all to an ideal of efficiency that abstracts from, and ultimately discards as valueless, what is most deeply and fragilely human in us.

L'Arche – communities of contrast

This contrast between community and society may not always be equally strongly felt by the assistants, particularly if they are from outside France, since the intensity of life in L'Arche homes quickly becomes so familiar as not to seem in any way remarkable. But from the perspective of someone like myself, with one foot in the community, and the other in the outside world of my work, the contrast seems not only evident, but importantly constitutive of L'Arche's identity.

There are, however, over 100 L'Arche communities throughout the world, and not all of them present this contrast with society 'outside' that I find in my own. In the developing world, for example – in countries such as India, Honduras and Haiti – the location of L'Arche communities reflects a deliberate decision to identify with the general social condition, by identification with those whose poverty is not merely material. And anyone who has visited more than one L'Arche community in any of the countries of the northern hemisphere knows that each has its own distinct identity, and that this is fortunate, since not everyone will find any particular community to his or her taste. But it remains true that what is prophetic in L'Arche is a sort of inversion of the values and aspirations of the social world, so that the communities, if they are faithful to their vocation, will proclaim or express an identity that contrasts with important and powerful forces at work in the surrounding society. The absence of this contrast is a sign that the life-giving roots are in danger of becoming dessiccated, and the vocation specific to L'Arche lost to view.

L'Arche as refuge?

If this seems no more than stating the obvious, it is important to realise that the idea that communites like L'Arche have a distinct identity encounters difficulties that emerge from both the theory and the practice of modern societies. One objection might be, for example, that the constant emphasis on weakness, poverty and brokenness that is part of the distinctive vision of L'Arche, as well as of the daily experience of the assistants, constitutes not so much an identity as a refuge. In this perspective long-term members of L'Arche communities could be defined collectively as people who cannot assume the solitude, responsibilities and competition of life in modern industrial economies. For these are economies that demand, above all else, two qualities which, though by no means without value in the life of a community, are noticeably absent from what is distinctive in the vision I have just described: the need to be strong, forceful, assertive, on the one hand; and the need to be innovative, forward-looking and time-conscious on the other.

What emerges from considering these (no doubt valuable) qualities with those that are distinctive to life in a community is a contrast between diametrically opposed philosophies of human growth and flourishing. The idea that a consciousness of human weakness and fragility, and more particularly of one's own weakness and fragility, can be anything other than an excuse for morose introspection and self-pity is flatly rejected by the climate of competitive excellence necessary to the functioning of modern economies. It is rejected, too, in an even more profound way, by a constant emphasis on innovation and the need to be efficient with time: 'Never waste time', 'Time is money', 'Quality-time'; none of these formulas (and particularly the last, which is scarcely more than a mere euphemism) would in any way contradict or exclude the emphasis found at L'Arche on attentiveness to the needs of each person, and particularly to the poorest and weakest, were it not for the fact that time is conceived in the mentality of the industrialised, secularised West as always coming towards us or disappearing behind us. 'The literally present moment', says William James, 'is a purely verbal supposition; the only present ever realized concretely being the "passing moment" in which the dying rearward of time and its dawning future forever mix their lights'.[1]

The model of human flourishing proposed in contemporary society visibly favours some people over others: the strong over the weak; the resourceful and capable over the incapacitated. Society is, or should be, according to the values it proclaims, meritocratic. But the values that govern life in community are quite different, and it is no objection to them that they should be so. L'Arche owes its foundation, and its name, to the need to protect the vulnerable and create for them a climate of trust, confidence and growth quite different from the incarcerating institutions from which so many of them have come. In doing so, Father Thomas Philippe, Jean Vanier, and all those who have followed them, have made the discovery that the revelation of weakness is fundamental to a true understanding of what it is to be human, of what is common to all human beings, whatever their status in society: what is most authentically human, etymologically, is what is closest to the experiences of birth and death – namely, weakness and suffering. The paradox of L'Arche is to have revealed that this foundation is a source of joy and celebration, that true human growth and flourishing do not consist of a persistent and anxious consciousness of what is lost to the past or demanded by the future, but, as Jean Vanier so often says, in 'wasting' time with others.

L'Arche as social club?

A second objection to the idea that communities like L'Arche have a distinct and recognisable identity goes in the opposite direction. Whereas the first sees such communities as nothing more than a refuge, the second recognises no clear identity in them at all: a community from this perspective is merely an association of like-minded individuals who, though they have responsibility for those unable to do so, are themselves able to vote, travel, buy a house, and at any time leave the community for employment elsewhere. Members thus belong to the community, not as to a tribe or other self-governing social group for reasons of survival, but because they share its spiritual values and its collective sense of warmth and friendship. But there are countless examples of social groups of this kind in modern society, frequently, indeed usually, overlapping one another, with the result that the term 'community' becomes associated with such a variety of different sub-groups in society that it ceases to have any specific meaning.

It is nevertheless true that communities such as L'Arche are not self-sufficient. They depend financially upon the state, and must respect the laws and customs of the society of which they are a part. But more important still, the very nature and distinctive qualities of this type of community depend – unlike the rural communes and feudal hierarchies of pre-modern societies – on the free and unconstrained, mature commitment of their members. It is important to recognise that this freedom is, at its root, individualistic, in the sense made clear by Charles Taylor,[2] of creating for the individual the social space in which to pursue his or her authentic vision of flourishing and self-development. If, however, the freedoms of the individual which lie at the foundation of modern, industrialised, liberal democracies are equally basic to the authenticity of life in community, in what way can the latter be seen as having a distinct 'identity', still less one opposed to or contrasting with the former?

The answer to this question is that, although these freedoms are basic to and necessary to both, they are insufficient to define the identity of community. Communities do require the free commitment of their members, and indeed require of them a measure of internal independence that would have been inconceivable without the emergence of modern individualism: 'In our society,' says Taylor, 'no one seems to be induced to participate in community life through a *lack* of private space'.[3] But the whole is not, as contemporary social theory postulates of the wider society, an aggregate of equal (and often competing) liberties. The freedom to commit oneself to life in community is only a point of departure; it is not the aim of living together. Instead, a deeper and qualitatively different dimension to liberty emerges in community – a liberty to grow and become oneself, to develop gifts and potentialities that cannot easily emerge in a competitive environment, those that are most authentically one's own, those that finally bridge the gulf (as Karl Marx had dreamed) between what I can give and what others need. This may not, and often does not, happen – or at least, not in the rather idealised way just described. But the distinctive quality of community is to propose a model of growth and flourishing which at least permits the uncovering and collective recognition of such capacities.

Contemporary Western societies and 'freedom'

Since the experience of the totalitarian regimes of the mid-twentieth century, liberal political philosophers have been almost unanimously hostile to any suggestion that genuine liberty can in any way go beyond the minimal, 'negative' freedoms of citizenship in modern societies. 'Positive' freedom, or the idea that there can be some connection between the social whole and the moral psychology of the individual, has been seen as necessarily curtailing or suppressing the sovereign right of individuals to choose (and consequently to re-evaluate the choice of) their own ends. The methodological separation of 'self' from 'ends' has thus come to be seen as essential to the preservation of liberty as such, and to postulate a 'dominant end' (in the expression of John Rawls[4]) – i.e., a single, unified vision of life in which choices and commitments are ordered hierarchically – would be to violate that liberty and remove the possibility of an individual's developing as he or she chooses. 'Traditional' or pre-modern society, by contrast, was authoritarian, not so much in the pejorative sense of being despotic, but in the sense, made clear by Hannah Arendt in her essay, 'What is authority?',[5] of depending for its legitimation on a hierarchy of meaning that transcended the mere exercise of power. Authority correctly understood, she says, rests neither upon the exercise of force, nor upon reasoned discussion between equals, but upon the pre-existence of this hierarchy to which the person exercising authority and the person obeying each belong. The disappearance of this kind of social hierarchy, and the social atrophy of the religious traditions with which it co-existed, have resulted not merely, according to Hannah Arendt, in the loss of the sense of authority, but in an enfeebling of liberty.

The explanation of this paradox emerges once it is understood that social philosophy has traditionally always included the philosophical evaluation of the ends of government and society. It is this which has always given it its recognisably ethical dimension. The 'means' for the attainment of those ends included the different types of institutional organisation compatible with the 'end' in view. What has emerged since the Enlightenment, however, has been an inversion of this traditional relationship between ends and means, so that democratic institutions – the economic mechanism of the free market and the jurisprudential sufficiency of the rule of law – are now taken for granted as the (much more modest) ends to be pursued, and a rational discussion of the ultimate ends of society has become no more possible than an evaluation of the 'purpose' of nature. A society, in this perspective, is no more than the sum of its parts, its purposes no more than the sum total of the individual purposes of its citizens. To attribute to the social whole, or to the ideal–typical individual who is part of it, any ultimate purpose (or *telos*) is to commit the double sin of imagining dubious metaphysical entities where none exists, and transgressing the democratic right of each individual to choose and re-choose for himself or herself which ultimate ends to pursue. Few people can be in any doubt that this inversion of perspective has enabled liberal democracies to avoid many very real social and political evils, but not without a price: for it is not merely a question of devaluing ends in favour of means – the means themselves (democracy, for example) have come to be seen as the only ends that can meaningfully be pursued by men and women collectively. And there results a sort of telescoping of moral purposes, a 'foreshortening of our ethical horizons', that has had an important part in the 'disenchanting' of the world, depriving it of moral oxygen as it were, paradoxically just as the liberties of individuals were being extended so significantly.

Three common tendencies in contemporary Western societies

1. Proceduralism

The process just described goes a long way towards explaining the centrality of three tendencies common to contemporary liberal political philosophies, as well as to the liberal–democratic societies of which they are an attempt to give normative shape and justification. The first, unsurprisingly, is a preoccupation with *procedures*. In the absence of any shared substantive conception, and hierarchical ranking, of social goods, what become central to society are neutral procedural arrangements whose purpose is to channel and resolve the conflicts that inevitably result from the simultaneous pursuit of incommensurable goods. The most visible of these procedures is representative democracy, and philosophers such as Marcel Gauchet and Claude Lefort sing the praises of its moral indeterminacy, of the 'void' at the heart of a democratic society, that is the individual's ultimate protection against tyranny: 'A democratic society,' says

Gauchet, 'is one which produces its own legitimacy within itself, by its internal functioning'.[6] That this legitimacy does not represent an equally strong ideal in the minds of everyone has been evident ever since the emergence of mass democracy revealed considerable levels of apathy and indifference in voting patterns, prompting a debate during the 1950s over the 'usefulness' of political apathy. It is most unlikely that anyone would want to defend political apathy today: levels of disaffection are so dangerously high, and the sense of moral disorientation so great (particularly among the young), that there is a felt urgency in the task of somehow recovering or reintroducing a substantive ('strong') moral dimension to democracy. But it is not easy to see how this could be done, for as liberals typically (and correctly) reply, it is a mistake to look to democracy itself to give meaning to our lives: instead, it provides unparalleled opportunities for individuals to find for themselves the meaning that best suits them at the level of associative life – the public realm is essentially neutral.

2. Individualism

Perhaps the most widely discussed aspect of contemporary society is its individualism. But this protean and much debated word does not fully translate the peculiar quality of what, for want of a better term, I shall call 'social negativity'. What I mean is the way in which modern societies depend for their stability on an equilibrium of centrifugal forces. These forces are not merely individual: they are frequently collective (ethnic, religious, political, commercial, therapeutic), and intersect confusingly with the concept of community, so that we find ourselves speaking of 'local' communities, ethnic communities, therapeutic communities, national communities.[7] There is, in other words, an irreducible pluralism, in terms of both ideals and social attachments, that characterises late modernity; but it is a highly fluid and unstable pluralism, rendering the philosophical understanding of the identity of individuals, 'selves', and consequently of their collective ethical commitments, deeply problematic. In such a climate, it is scarcely surprising that the most widely shared characteristic of individuals should be a fear of commitment to any non-provisional relationship or set of relationships.

As a consequence, recent political philosophy has set itself the task of elaborating sets of devices whose purposes, while diverse, all express, in one form or another, the need to accommodate the fears of the individual: the fear of one's rights being denied by the state; the fear of having to make one's lifestyle conform to the prejudices of the majority; the fear that one's cultural specificity will be diluted; the fear of exclusion from the collective benefits resulting from economic growth; and so on. And given the scale and complexity of modern industrial states, and the violence of the clashes of interests that characterise their normal functioning, these fears are clearly well-founded, and the demand for reassurance legitimate. Fear, then, seems to be the necessary basic component of any social philosophy on a scale matching that of modern society as a whole.[8]

Despite the fact that this emptiness and the centrality of fear mentioned above do not in any profound way account for the social aspirations of a significant proportion of the citizens of modern states, the danger of a sort of moral 'implosion' has until now been avoided by the liberal faith in 'progress', i.e. the benefits of sustainable economic growth and the transformative power of technology. But ever since the 1960s, this faith has been called into question, and the collapse of the liberal West's chief ideological adversary seems, paradoxically, to have precipitated a generalised crisis of confidence, a sense of the ultimate meaninglessness even of progress quantitively understood, that appears to vindicate the nihilistic diagnoses offered by Max Weber at the end of the first world war.[9]

3. Materialism

In his studies of the emergence of modern from traditional society, the French anthropologist Louis Dumont has shown how the emergence of individualism is accompanied by a profound and important change in the way a society conceives of wealth.[10] In traditional, agrarian societies there exists a clear distinction, reflecting their relative importance, between land ('immovable' wealth) and 'mobile' (e.g. capital) wealth: rights over land, because they reflect rights over men, are of infinitely greater value, are intrinsically superior, to the ownership of capital (or any other type of wealth which is movable), which is despised as a mere relation to 'things'. In the modern world this link between landed wealth and political power has been broken, creating, among other things, the distinct categories of 'politics' and 'economics' with which we are familiar today. But the most important consequence for our purpose here is that the dynamic, central relationship in modern societies is no longer that between men and men (a relationship maintained by the hierarchical nature of the pre-modern social order, the rights and obligations of whose members were related to the ownership of land), but between people and *things*. Relationships between people are, as Dumont says, 'subordinated' to relationships of material ownership.

What I have just said should not be misunderstood: it is not that interpersonal relationships are unimportant in modern society, still less that they are impossible; but in the context of free-market economies, they are no longer *dynamic* in shaping the structure and institutions that organise our lives. They have secondary, instrumental importance in a perspective that sees the growth and equitable distribution of capital wealth as fundamental. Such a change has consequences for the freedom of human persons – consequences which are not perceived if we attend only to equality and rights. If, in pre-modern society, I could be a fully human being only by freeing myself from ownership by others, in modern society my autonomy depends on my being able to distinguish the boundary between myself and my possessions and desires. This dilemma is strikingly expressed by Michael Sandel in the following passage from his book *Liberalism and the Limits of Justice*:

> To preserve the distinction between what is me and what is merely mine, I must know, or be able to sort out when the occasion demands, something about who I am ... I gradually lose possession of a thing, not only as it is distanced from my person, but also as the distance between myself and the thing narrows and tends towards collapse. I lose possession of a desire

or an ambition as my commitment to it fades, as my hold on it becomes more attenuated, but also, after a certain point, as my attachment to it grows, as it gradually becomes attached to me. As the desire or ambition becomes increasingly constitutive of my identity, it becomes more and more me and less and less mine.[11]

The uncertain relationship Sandel describes between personal identity and desires and ambitions has no doubt always existed. What is perhaps specific to modernity is the way in which the perspective of desire–fulfilment 'liquidates the past', creating a world where particular attachments to tradition and community (understood in the broadest sense) are counted as irrational, and where 'only the future counts'.[12]

Communities and traditions

If the relevant characteristics of contemporary Western societies are as just described (i.e. that they depend for their legitimacy on a weak, procedurally-generated conception of public good, that their institutions reflect the fear that is a consequence of their underlying individualism, and that their central, dynamic relationship is between people and things), might we not expect a communitarian philosophy, opposed root and branch to this impoverished vision of the social world, to advocate a return to a 'thick' theory of social good, a restored social holism and the primacy of interpersonal relationships?

The answer to this question is a qualified 'yes' – qualified because community is not merely, and in most ways not at all, a return to the past, to a *status quo ante*. And if the question, 'What do communities like L'Arche have to offer people living in a world like this?' is taken to mean what global solutions can they offer, then the answer is clearly: none. Much of the writing by philosophical communitarians, having begun from the modest (and praiseworthy) recognition of the need to resituate the identity of the subject at the level of the life of the actual cultures and subcultures of contemporary societies (and thereby collapse the distance between 'selves' and 'ends'), has discredited itself by appearing to advocate a return to tribalism and relativism, and the consequent abandonment of any possibility of a rational discussion of ethical questions. Communities, like communitarian philosophy, cannot attempt to resolve all the contradictions of liberal individualism without endangering both liberalism and individuality. Communities which depend for their identity on a deeply authoritarian (in the pejorative sense) mode of functioning end up – as so often happens among house churches – as tiny sectarian tyrannies. Extremes of individualism and sectarianism, as post-Reformation history shows, are mutually reinforcing. Here, though, lie the beginnings of an answer: for the different Christian confessions have managed to survive the spread of the secularised, predominantly economic, individualism of the modern world, thanks to the development and enrichment of their respective traditions. Traditions, as Alasdair MacIntyre says, are 'bearers of reason'.[13] Communities, if they are to avoid the very real dangers of sectarianism, must adhere deeply, humbly, to the religious traditions of their members: deeply, because traditions are a source of life; humbly, because they are broader and older than the communities they enrich and guide. A readiness to submit to an authority outside itself (i.e. a tradition) is what makes possible the distinction between a community and a sect: sects are not, in the first place, distinguished by their deliberate desire to distort the truth (that comes later) – but by their spiritual pride, by their refusal of human weakness and by their exaggeration of the importance of certain truths at the expense of others. The intense and searching exposure of human frailty, especially the (very obvious) frailties of the confessional traditions just referred to, is extremely seductive in a world with a thirst for authenticity and integrity. If traditions are bearers of reason, it is a reason incarnated in human frailty – and they are enriched, in their turn, by a deepened understanding of that frailty.

Traditions do not necessarily give life: they can stagnate and suffocate as much as vivify. And even if they are alive and life-giving, they cannot of themselves account for the emergence of the 'new' communities that have spread across the world (and very strikingly across France) since the 1960s. If traditions alone sufficed we would not need communities: our different confessional traditions would be sufficient. The strength and originality of the new communities have instead given new life to these traditions, and they have done so by uncovering (as opposed to recovering) dimensions of human collective life masked or obscured by the proceduralism, individualism and materialism of contemporary societies.

The recovery of narrative

Communities have done this, in the first place, by uncovering a deeper, richer meaning to the term 'authority' than the pejorative caricature with which its liberal critics tax philosophical communitarianism. Since human beings are, in Alasdair MacIntyre's phrase, 'story-telling animals',[14] they discover the meaning of their lives not through rights or procedures, but through narratives. For it is narratives that give unity to a human life by uniting a person's past with his or her present, and by conceiving the future, not in terms of a chaos of undifferentiated desires, but in relation to that past and this present, growing out of them towards ends which, though deeply personal, are also shared. Although the 'authorship' of these narratives lies ultimately with the persons whose narratives they are, the collective narrative that concerns the birth and growth to maturity of the communites within which men and women can, at last, uncover this narrative dimension of their lives requires an *authority*: an authority in the two Latin senses of *auctor*, an originator,[15] and *augere*, to give growth. Like the monastic communities founded in the Middle Ages, the new communities have identifiable founders, most of whom are still alive, and whose importance lies not only in communicating their vision but in accompanying and encouraging each member of the community in finding unity in his or her life. Both of these dimensions are lived at L'Arche in a quite explicit way: the narrative dimension of the community as a whole is continually revived by recounting the early beginnings of L'Arche's history; and the individual narrative of each member is celebrated and evoked at birthdays and celebrations of ten years spent with the community.

The recovery of the narrative dimension of human life is important because it unifies: the past to the present, the weaknesses to the strengths, the failures and setbacks to the successes and triumphs. More deeply still, it serves to integrate death, suffering, loss, into the life of which they are a part. Society as a whole necessarily excludes this process of integration from the picture of the human subject integral to its functioning, since any reminder of the inevitability (still less the value and importance) of weakness, suffering and failure would detract from the forward dynamic of expansion and innovation. But nor can the isolated individual give full sense and meaning to the narrative dimension of his or her life, since the celebration of a person's narrative is a quintessentially social or collective occasion, but one whose only outlets in society are weddings and funerals. It is true that psychoanalysis exists as a way of restoring narrative unity to the life of the subject – but what it singularly lacks is the dimension of celebration, of joy. The celebration of a person's often long and incomplete struggle to bring unity to the story of his or her life is instead the task of community.

The recovery and celebration, through community, of the narrative dimension of human life helps to counteract the second of the social tendencies identified above – the institutional centrality of fear. For narratives include ends in the sense both of purposes and of conclusions: the uncovering of narratives leads to the recovery of purposes – purposes which, if understood in an Aristotelian perspective, are shared. Community is built upon the foundation of a common desire to live together, based, unlike sects and the individualism that secretes them, upon a common sensitivity to human weaknesses. True, as with any social group, much accommodation is necessary, and it is not necessarily any less conflictual in community than in society at large. But a community has an end in view, a *telos*, which is both personal and shared. The foundations of community, as Pierre-Marie Delfieux says,[16] lie in the co-existence of collective unity and an authentic and courageously assumed personal solitude, the realisation of which is inescapably theological because it is a reflection of the doctrine of the Trinity. People who live in communities are not there as a result of professional obligations: they choose to build the whole of which they are a part, and in doing so accept that their obligations towards it are more than merely utilitarian.

The meeting of persons

But more than to the whole, the obligations that are dynamic to the life of communities are obligations to persons. What is specific to L'Arche, however, is to reveal that obligations (such as charity and generosity) fail to meet or to encounter the person in front of me in a relationship of communion. For communion is not, like an obligation, a relationship contracted on the basis of some event in the past; nor does it, like the generosity of the benefactor, seek above all to 'make something' of the person benefited.[17] It is possible instead only in what Father Thomas Philippe used to call 'the thickness of the present moment'. It is possible only if I shed my desires, expectations, projections and perhaps, above all, my conviction that I have something to bring or offer the person in front of me apart from my own simple, impoverished self. I arrived at L'Arche, as many others have arrived before and since, my anxieties and trepidation masked by an appearance of socially acceptable rationality, and found myself confronted with people whose chaos was all on the 'outside' – exuberant, unembarrassed and above all unafraid of me. The confrontation was only a confrontation from my perspective: from that of the men and women with handicaps who welcomed me it was an invitation to remove my masks and begin the inner journey towards wholeness whose starting-point cannot be our strengths (which are too weak) but our weaknesses. Ten years on, I am not certain of having made much progress (perhaps because for most of that time I have only had one foot in the community!), but at the same time I am certain that I could not have made what little progress I have without the strength of the community.

L'Arche, in common with other communities, is (among many other things) an invitation to live without masks. But we have to *learn* to live without masks, and the process is painful and never complete (fortunately, since the disappearance of all opacity would be terrifying). It is made easier by the discovery of the infinite value of the poorest, least efficient, most dis-abled men and women – people whose disabilities are a sign that it is not being able that makes us human. It is from them that we can learn that authentic human relationships are neither merely inherited from the past, nor autonomously chosen or constructed towards ends which are individual: they are given to us in the degree to which we become open to the discovery of what is weakest and most vulnerable in ourselves, and in others.

Part II

Reflections on L'Arche
and its significance
for the
Christian tradition

L'ARCHE AND JESUS:
WHAT IS THE THEOLOGY?

DAVID F. FORD

For David Ford, 'part of the provocative witness of L'Arche is its following Jesus by living in the face of death'. He takes themes: the cross, the face of Christ, gentleness, vocation, singing and the Eucharist. In each case, L'Arche both challenges our culture and intensifies reflection on the Christian tradition.

I have been gripped by L'Arche. As a theologian I have found that, in the face of those who often cannot articulate thought, thought is intensified. For me it has resonated with the experience of two severely disabled members of my family: my Aunt Cora, who spent many years in Cheshire Homes in Dublin; and my nephew and godson Conal, who was living in a Steiner community when he died, aged 17, in a fire he had started himself. I do not know L'Arche very well, however; what follows are initial thoughts on a theme that deserves far fuller treatment, and also calls for a more thorough engagement with the L'Arche communities – which I hope will come later.

Familiar with death

'We are familiar with death here', said Jean Vanier at our group's first gathering in L'Arche, Trosly-Breuil, in 1993. At the meeting in 1995, Antonio was dying, and I spent some time by his bedside as he lay hooked up to drips, his birthday presents piled on the bed. Life went on as usual in the household around him, and yet it was clear that Antonio would soon be dead. This was realistically faced – but at the same time, life in Antonio's presence seemed more vibrant. Jean said of him: 'It is beautiful but dangerous to live with him: he demands a lot of presence'. He was being given that presence, and the result was a dying that seemed like the fulfilment of a vocation.

We demand a lot of presence from God – to the point of crucifixion. Jesus is portrayed as having a vocation to die, and he lived with an unrepressed sense of death, familiar with it. That was scandalous then, and it may be even more so now. So much in our Western culture fears death, denies it, represses it, sees it as the opposite of life and the worst that can happen to anyone. Many people regard severe disability as something like a living death, and so the condition shares something of death's disgrace. Disability, like death, gives a different perspective on many of the idols of our culture: success, comfort, health, being in control, sex, power. So part of the provocative witness of L'Arche is its following Jesus by living vibrantly in the face of death. The household sang daily as Antonio lay there. The way of Jesus to crucifixion and resurrection enabled the community to face death and disability in a certain spirit, blending utter realism with hope and joy.

The painful presence which our condition demands of God is not an instant solution to our problems. As Peter Harvey said at the 1993 meeting: 'Christianity is not so much problem-solving as mystery-encountering'. The mystery of the death of Jesus Christ generates endless reflection as it grips deeper and deeper. Jesus Christ's death 'for us' does not solve the 'problem' of death, nor does it prevent people from being disabled or having to die. It rather creates a community which can remember his death and resurrection, and in the light of that can refuse to repress or run away from suffering, evil or death. Resurrection is not an escape from life and death, but a sending deeper into life that which has been baptised in death. That life is in a community which is energised by the same Spirit that led Jesus Christ along the way of the cross, and so is inevitably involved in painful presence.

The 'for us' is, therefore, not a substitute in the sense of not requiring our involvement; on the contrary, Jesus' death is in order to involve us utterly. So Antonio's death revealed a community following a vocation of painful presence, and Antonio following his vocation (unimaginable apart from the community) of truly living in the face of death. The overall effect was that death as an impersonal, irresistible, fearsome force was denied. Instead, there was no doubt of the central reality: it was Antonio's remarkable face, with large, deep brown eyes. Baptism into the death of Christ means that now death does not have the last word. Rather, the human face on the cross, the face of one who died and rose, is the truth of death. The mark of the cross on each particular face in baptism is united with a particular name, and that marks the face as the ultimate reality: 'Now we see through a glass darkly, but then face to face' (1 Cor. 13:12, RSV). 'We all, with unveiled face, beholding [or reflecting] the glory of the Lord, are being changed into his likeness from one degree of glory to another; for this comes from the Lord who is the Spirit' (2 Cor. 3:18). That likeness into which we are being transformed includes death, and Paul goes on to talk of 'always carrying in our bodies the death of Jesus, so that the life of Jesus may also be manifested in our bodies' (2 Cor. 4:10). The mutual reflecting of glory that was going on between Antonio and his community is a testimony that challenges the dictatorial power of death over so many areas of life, and is a subversive sign of the kingdom of God. It is possible to have worthwhile life and even joy by living together without what our culture regards as success – status, comfort, health, being in control, sexual satisfaction or power.

The face of Christ

I am fascinated by the face of Christ. It is a mystery that gets richer as time goes by. When Frances Young and I spent years together writing a book on Paul's second letter to the Corinthians, we found that the most significant verse in the letter was: 'For it is the God who said, "Light will shine out of darkness," who has shone in our hearts to give the light of the knowledge of the glory of God in the face of Christ' (4:6, my translation). Paul goes on to say: 'But we have this treasure in earthen vessels, to show that the transcendent power belongs to God and not to us' (4:7). The treasure of that face shining in the heart is the essence of Jesus' good news; and the power of it is all the greater when its container is weak, 'afflicted in every way' (4:8), carrying death.

The glory of that face can be glimpsed in many ways. It offers a path through the Gospels, where most of the stories are of face-to-face encounters. The meditations are infinite: on Mary's face touching Jesus; on his immersion in the Jordan in baptism; on his encounters in teaching, healing, meals and hostility; on the face 'shining like the sun' in the transfiguration; on Jesus' anointing with oil; on his eating and drinking at the Last Supper; the face prostrate on the ground, sweating blood in Gethsemane, then receiving Judas' kiss; the face wearing the crown of thorns; the apocryphal Veronica wiping Jesus's face on the way to Golgotha; the face in agony, crying out, and dead; the mysterious resurrection appearances with their strangeness and yet recognition; the breathing of the Holy Spirit face to face; the blessing with pierced hands as Jesus ascends. Finally, there is the orientation of those who live in faith towards seeing the Lord 'face to face'.

All that suggests a particular face, the unique central character of one story. But this was not a face that asked for attention to itself. Jesus looked to God and to other people. To meditate on his face is to find our gaze being drawn where his is directed: towards God and, inseparably, towards our neighbours. This is a self-effacing face. It shines through a life lived for others and for God. Being faced by Jesus means radical welcome, dignity, being loved. The main problem then becomes how to cope with being loved like this. The solution is beautifully simple: one copes by returning love to him – which means to God and to other people. In fact, the deepest truth about seeing the face of Jesus might be that his is now a face in self-distribution. Having died for all, he looks on all in love, and our way of glimpsing him is face by face by face, in our brothers and sisters who are loved by him. As we really see them, in their dignity in the image of God, we appreciate the 'glory of God in the face of Christ'. That is such a superabundant glory that if every face in the world were reflecting some of it there would still be infinite scope for being transformed 'from one degree of glory to another' (2 Cor. 3:18). And the converse of that is also crucial: if we want to know the glory of that face, we cannot ignore any human face. The call of the face of Christ is to 'demanding presence' before each other, rooted in amazed gratitude that we ourselves are living before such presence. The first letter of Peter is written to 'the exiles of the Dispersion', who are undergoing great hardship, about being orientated towards 'the revelation of Jesus Christ. Without having seen him you love him; though you do not now see him you believe in him and rejoice with unutterable and exalted joy' (1:7f.).

L'Arche is a place where the dynamics of faces in relationship seem especially significant. 'The hardest thing is when people behave as if you're not there', said Thérèse Vanier quoting a disabled friend. Society mostly does behave like that towards the disabled, seeing their disability, not their face. L'Arche is a place where helpers and disabled can learn to see the face. At the very least that means that disability ceases to fill the whole horizon: faces, not problems, are the main focus. It may be that 'problems' and 'issues' are our greatest idols of all. The media are full of them, our lives are overwhelmed by them, and they suck in our attention, energies and resources like voracious false gods. Only a greater imperative can liberate us from such addiction and idolatry. The Jewish thinker, Emmanuel Levinas, found such an imperative in the face of the other person, where we meet a radical summons to responsibility: he spoke of the 'hospitality of the face'. In L'Arche one glimpses some of the dimensions of that hospitality.

One striking feature is the discovery of the sort of beauty that only comes from being looked on with love, from being appreciated and delighted in, over a long time. Katharine Hall, at our 1995 meeting, spoke of 'waiting for the beauty' – it may take years, and you may have to have your eyes opened to a new sort of beauty; but it happens, time and time again – and always differently. The face is by no means the only aspect of this, but it is the most intense focus of communication, individuality and human beauty. Tzvi Marx, in his magisterial treatment of Jewish approaches to disability, tells of a Jewish tradition of saying a benediction on meeting someone with a disability, his favourite being that of Rabbi Joshua ben Levi:

'Blessed be he who makes creatures different'.[1] Enhancing the dignity of difference, and even its beauty, is at the heart of our responsibility for each other before the face of God.

'I am gentle'

The face is not just seen, it is touched and touches. 'My face touching Loïc's face awakens something deep' (Jean Vanier). Touching is a primary form of communication in L'Arche. It flows through the day – in dressing, eating, carrying, hair-care, bathing, playing, and just keeping in touch. It is another very sensitive area in our culture, and not one to be naïve about. But its fundamental element seems to me to be gentleness. Might gentleness be a vital prophetic virtue for our period? The violence of our times is horrendous – physical violence, verbal violence, economic violence, structural and institutional violence, spiritual violence. This is intensified by its being vividly represented in the media, so that violence often dominates imaginations.

Jesus' statement, 'I am gentle' (Matt. 11:29, my translation), follows on from his beatitude: 'Blessed are the gentle, for they shall inherit the earth' (Matt. 5:5). In the rest of the New Testament, gentleness appears as one of a small family of interrelated qualities. The list in Galatians 5:22–3 is: 'Love, joy, peace, patience, kindness, goodness, faithfulness, gentleness and self-control'. Ephesians urges leading a life 'with all lowliness and gentleness, with patience, forbearing one another in love, eager to maintain the unity of the Spirit in the bond of peace' (4:2–3), and soon afterwards says: 'Be kind to one another, tenderhearted, forgiving one another, as God in Christ forgave you' (4:32). Each of those virtues involves the others, and I will take gentleness as a focus for them – and one which has special relevance to L'Arche and to our culture.

Gentleness is usually practised, if at all, as an optional extra, as something peripheral and secondary. It is nothing short of a revolution to imagine it at the heart not only of individuals but of groups and institutions. But might that be part of the implication of Jesus' beatitude? Is it conceivable? I know two vivid examples of the possibilities.

The first is Broadmoor Hospital in England. It is a 'secure hospital' for the criminally insane, and many of the crimes that led to patients being sent there made shocking headlines. The chief psychotherapist, Dr Murray Cox, has over some years arranged for the Royal Shakespeare Company to perform at Broadmoor. In 1996 Mark Rylance came with an *ad hoc* company to give the last performance of their production of *Macbeth*. My wife and I were there for the superb presentation, which was followed by a discussion of the play between the patients and the cast. We also met some of the psychotherapists there, as well as other staff-members – the hospital employs more staff than it has patients. The security was intense, with endless locked doors, cameras, massive high walls, and some extremely alert, fit and tough-looking 'nurses' in track-suits.

My own key insight occurred as we came away from the play through all the security, and looked up at the walls: within all this toughness there was gentleness – people had watched drama sensitively performed; but above all they were *talked with*. There was no sentimentality or indulgence, and the danger of the criminally insane was taken seriously; but, nevertheless, at the heart of it, capable professionals were paid to take time, year after year, to talk, to understand, and to help patients face themselves and other people in the aftermath of their crimes.

There was a sharp contrast immediately afterwards in the taxi to the station: the driver, in the course of a short ride, was scornful of the 'cushy life' these patients had, and in three different ways he said that if he had his way he would exterminate them all. I suspect too that if there were a vote among taxpayers, he might find a good deal of support. I do not at all want to idealise Broadmoor; but it is clear that, in contrast with comparable institutions 100 years ago, there has been a move towards greater gentleness, exemplified in long-term psychotherapy. Whatever the results of this treatment (and I understand the staff are often encouraged), there is here a costly affirmation of human dignity in people who are easy to write off.

The second example is L'Arche, where the ethos of gentleness might be seen as the *raison d'être* of the whole institution. Again, there is little sentimentality and there can be appropriate firmness and even toughness. Violence too is a threat. 'The screams of anguish awakened great violence in me. Because I was in community I was held. But parents of the disabled are frequently alone' (Jean Vanier). Helpers and disabled are tested to their limits, and it is clear that for gentleness to thrive it has to be sustained institutionally. Gentleness at the core has consequences for the way the organisation is run, and how power is distributed and used. To call this a 'fruit of the Spirit' is to say that it is a sign of the real presence of Jesus Christ, but a sign that can never be secured: it is had by daily appeal to the one who said 'I am gentle', and who promised appropriate power for practising gentleness and its kindred qualities. But it is not only Jesus: it is Jesus and Mary. 'Gentle' is one of the commonest attributes ascribed to Mary, and it is no accident that devotion to Mary goes very deep in L'Arche. One of the contributors to this book, Donald Allchin, has written a book about Mary in my own Anglican tradition.[2] He sees her affirming the importance of the body in a faith which is in practice often 'unbelievably discarnate', and doing so through inspiring tenderness as an ideal for men as well as women.

It is hard to exaggerate the extent to which our culture puts toughness at the centre, and is uncomprehending or scornful of gentleness beyond certain very limited spheres: in some practices of courtesy; in sexual foreplay (though many images of sex are shot through with violence); with animals; and especially with children (but even there fears of abuse are paralysing freedom of touch). The economics of the market is perhaps the main influence, stressing the 'bottom line', ruthless pursuit of profit and efficiency, the commodification and pricing of everything, and that admired hero, the 'tough businessman'. It is not at all enough to complain about this (and it is worth recognising that other cultures have had their analogous ways of marginalising gentleness). It is rather a matter of a twofold thrust: to modify existing institutions in the direction of greater gentleness, as in Broadmoor; and to engage in the sort of institutional creativity that is seen in L'Arche, where, in relation to people who are often rejected, ignored, or treated unfeelingly and merely as problems, a prophetic, hopeful alternative is developed with gentleness at the core.

Vocation

After yearning for a host of vocations St Thérèse of Lisieux finally discovered it: 'My vocation is love!' But what does her 'my' mean? Love means a transformation of self: others become intrinsic to who one is, and in loving that means being loved. Perhaps the most difficult thing of all is learning to be loved. The thrust of Thérèse's call is towards its being primarily joint vocation. An isolated call to love and be loved is unimaginable. That is very much the biblical sense of vocation too: the call of Abraham is inseparable from the call of a people; the election of Israel is the context for the vocations of its kings, judges, prophets, priests, parents and ordinary worshipping people. The image of the Church as a body reinforces this: hands and feet do not have separate vocations. L'Arche intensifies it yet further, because half of its members could not lead what are known as independent lives. Theirs is a vocation which makes highly visible their dependence upon others; but in terms of a vocation of love, there is no relation of dependency: there is utter reciprocity with the helpers – each in a household or community is intrinsic to the vocation of the others. And as has often been noticed, this sort of community fosters richer individuality: people become more themselves, their faces more full of life, and new beauty appears. The category of vocation is one which can do justice both to the calling of a community and to the endlessly varied individual stories which are woven together there. When it is seen through the vocation of Jesus to suffering and death, it relativises all disability: all suffer the disability of death, but vocation does not stop there.

Singing

Joint vocation is realised in all sorts of ways. I want to conclude with one expression of it that occurs every day in any L'Arche community: singing together. 'And when they had sung a hymn, they went out to the Mount of Olives' (Mark 14:26). Jesus sang with his disciples as he faced death. Singing was clearly deeply embedded in the life of the early Church. One of the most vivid illustrations is the encouragement in Ephesians 5:18–21:

> Do not get drunk with wine, for that is debauchery; but be filled with the Spirit, as you sing psalms and hymns and spiritual songs among yourselves, singing and making melody to the Lord in your hearts, giving thanks to God the Father at all times and for everything, in the name of our Lord Jesus Christ, being subject to one another out of reverence for Christ.

I think that could be seen as a key to the whole letter. It acts out the first chapter's pervasive emphasis on 'the praise of God's glory', and the second chapter's picturing of the Church as a holy temple – the classic place for singing God's praise. The last sentence about being subject to one another is closely linked in the text both with what comes before it and what comes after – instructions for households, and the key relationships of husbands and wives, parents and children, masters and slaves. That conjures up a vision of singing households, relationships formed in an atmosphere of singing thanks. It also suggests a musical meaning for 'being subject to one another'. In singing, each needs to be sensitive to the others, to adjust to how the overall song is being sung. Power is fundamentally about the energy for attentive attunement to each other and, beyond that, to the music and words in which all are sharing.

Singing allows for many modes of participation. It can be full-voiced and articulate, hesitant and inarticulate, listening in silence, following the rhythm with fingers clicking or feet tapping or head bobbing, or energetic dancing. It can incorporate people while yet allowing for a wide range of responses. Its repetitive element gives participants the chance to grow into the music and the words, and to be formed by it over time. That formation can integrate body, mind and spirit. Often the body leads: one sings and the meaning follows later, often over a long period. This temporal dimension is vital. It is partly about habits which shape our time, and allow for a fresh relating of past, present and future. Think of the implications for our sense of time of the 'always and for everything giving thanks in the name of our Lord Jesus Christ to God the Father' of Ephesians 5:20: constant recapitulation of the past in singing before God is the way in which the future is approached. But, more than that, music transforms time itself. Music takes time, fills it and refigures it, offering 'new time' to live in. There is an intensification of life and energy through the sound of music which can resonate throughout the life of a community or an individual, and be a sacrament of their harmonious movement through time. Time itself is not some empty container, indifferent to what fills it. It is rather a relational reality whose potential for full life is glimpsed in singing to the Lord of all time. Nor is it an accident that the Ephesians passage is embraced within those fundamental relationships which the Church later came to distil intellectually in the doctrine of the Trinity: 'Be filled with the Spirit . . . giving thanks in the name of our Lord Jesus Christ to God the Father'.

Eucharistic time

The shaping of time is one of the most important aspects of culture, community and individual lives. L'Arche recognises this in all sorts of ways: in celebrating birthdays and anniversaries of coming to L'Arche; in the patterning of days, weeks and years; and above all in the rhythm of the liturgical year. But the heart of its sense of time is probably found in the celebration of the Eucharist (Donald Allchin writes about this in another essay in this volume). I want to conclude by noting how the elements I have selected for discussion all come together in the Eucharist. It is the normative Christian way of facing suffering and death without letting them have the last word. It is also about painful and joyful presence, and about a face-to-face relationship of eating, drinking and embracing. It focuses on the one whose 'I am gentle' was lived out in suffering violence, and in founding a community with a celebration of forgiveness at its heart. The very word 'eucharist' means thanks, and it is usually filled with singing. And it enacts perhaps the most basic of all senses of vocation: we are called to a meal. Those meals in the L'Arche households, often so messy, and the anticipation of the feast of the kingdom of God, are somehow focused together in those Eucharists in the converted barn in Trosly-Breuil. And high up above the altar is that little stained-glass window of a big owl with one wing embracing a little owl. Or is the little owl supporting the big owl's broken wing? Who is helping whom? Need we ask? It is the eyes that hold us above all.

ALONGSIDE L'ARCHE

Y. MOUBARAC

Youakim Moubarac approaches L'Arche from three perspectives. As a scholar of ancient Syrian traditions of asceticism, he interprets the encounter with persons who have profound mental disabilities as a new 'desert place' where one faces one's own interior demons. Then he allows L'Arche to challenge liberation theology. Finally he reflects on celibacy, and the way in which, freely accepted, it becomes at L'Arche a way of identification with those who had no choice, such as persons with disability.

What follows is not a personal testimony; rather, it is an attempt to interpret the experience which is lived out at L'Arche – an experience revealed to me in the course of friendship, which seems to have affected my thinking in three specific ways.

1. Reflections on desert places

As a researcher come late to the spirituality of Syrian Antioch, I was in the process of producing an introduction to it for use by Arabic readers. Among other ancient practices commended by all our Fathers and spiritual masters, I focused on that of absolute solitude as a unique way of developing attachment to God. But, I asked myself, is this ideal only accessible to a few? And assuming this to be the case, how will even those fitted to it fare in a world more and more urbanised, and where the desert places themselves are open to humankind's systematic exploitation of the planet?

It was then that I set myself to examine certain extreme states in modern existence. To such states as those of hospitalisation, imprisonment and confinement in concentration camps – states which typify extreme experiences that are becoming more and more widespread in the contemporary world – Jean Vanier has added the handicapped condition, and he has the audacity to think that it is a privileged place for meeting God. In his own way, Solzhenitsyn had already revealed this clearly in *Cancer Ward*, as had Pasternak in *Dr Zhivago*. More modestly, the founding literature of L'Arche seems to me to locate these great works within the current of the spiritual quest which makes Christianity converge with the very diverse ways which lead to God.

The literature of L'Arche seems to me to go even further, in having effected a decisive turn in the course of Christian spirituality and having radically resolved the tension between contemplation and action or apostolic life. In as far as I understand Jean Vanier, daily dealings with people who have handicaps makes those involved face their own violence. Confronted by the irreducibility of the other, the one whom they mean to serve but whose condition they cannot ameliorate, they discover with horror that they are capable of striking them, or even wanting to do away with them. It is this, then, that I call a privileged desert place. The ancient anchorites took themselves off to the desert, they said, to fight with Satan on his own territory. We know now that it is enough to pay attention to the most defenceless people among us to find ourselves given up to our interior demons. But if only we force ourselves not to lose heart, if only grace comes to the aid of our weakness, we apprehend that to spend time with the poorest of all is not to do them charity, but to allow ourselves to be transformed by them and to apprehend God as gentleness.

Jean Vanier's being present to profoundly handicapped people has taught me, not so much how to cope, as about the meaning and practice of this new desert place – desert in the sense of a space which confines us and limits, even as it exacerbates, our desire for distraction.

2. Reflections on liberation theology

The second effect of L'Arche on my thinking relates to what is usually called liberation theology. This theology has challenged me from the start because of the Arab–Israeli conflict and the religious motivations in which it is clothed. This has made me wary of every fusion of Christianity with the socio-economic, every amalgam of religion with politics. Acquaintance with L'Arche has only confirmed my existing views on this subject.

For all that, and speaking only for myself, I believe that to liberate my people I have no need to appeal to the holy Scriptures, but only to human rights. This is precisely what permits me to do so with the same motivations and on the same footing as non-Christians. By the same token, it is what allows me to disallow all political and military conflict which is improperly based on religion. In other words, secularisation should banish once for all the confusion of religious and political issues. Conversely, the gospel lays foundations for human rights – for both individuals and groups – with no regard for any ideology, and advocates the love of our enemies and that other love called preference for the poor.

So I believe that followers of Jean Vanier are justified in leaving each person to work out their reasons for fighting to achieve that justice, without which all peace is illusory. But such followers would be even nearer the truth if they reached the point of challenging all conflicts which did not first demand the honouring of those most needy, and did not make of their weakness the foundation of a new project for civilisation. As long as the poor – and among them those with handicaps – are those whom society helps rather than people at the heart of society's dynamic, as long as charity is a luxury for the privileged rather than an existential solidarity and effective sharing in the condition of people who are humiliated and spurned, the civilisations of which we claim to be part can proclaim whatever allegiances they wish – but not allegiance to the gospel.

3. Reflections on celibacy

The third and last way in which L'Arche affects my thinking concerns priestly celibacy – an ill-served subject in the debates of the contemporary Church. I would only say that, alongside the properly spiritual motivations which align the celibacy of Catholic priests with that of monks, I am looking for certain pastoral motivations, which relativise, or even brush aside, traditional discourse concerning the greater availability of unmarried clergy. Indeed, I perceive greater availability among the fathers and mothers of families, given that among celibates I find myself with a crowd of old bachelors who, with their inimitable masculine wiles, use women without offering anything in return, be she mother, aunt, housekeeper or religious sister.

So in searching not for monastic but for pastoral motivations for priestly celibacy, I have already discovered Gandhi's call to risk, and the theologian Moehler's struggle against power. One can only take risks for oneself alone, said Gandhi in his *Experiences with Truth*; and Moehler wrote to Pius IX saying that ecclesiastical celibacy must be safeguarded to enable the Church to stand up to the state. Only men freed from all family responsibilities could do this, Moehler suggested. With Jean Vanier, I discern a humbler, yet no less demanding, motivation. In approaching those who are most needy, we discover that they none the less require a total relationship; and the break-up of that relationship becomes for them a source of pain and frustration. The poorest are thus, for those who approach them, a call to that greater solitude long ago advocated by our spiritual Fathers and masters. So celibacy freely accepted becomes a way of identifying with those who have no choice, and by that mediation, communion with the one who revealed God between manger and cross as the most defenceless of all beings.

With reference to the manger and the cross, I ought to add that my knowledge of life at L'Arche comes from the private confidences of a Little Sister of Jesus. The above account results from considering her testimony alongside my researches into the spirituality of Syrian Antioch, and thus shows that the family of Charles de

Foucauld and Little Sister Magdalene had indeed got links with the East. And when Francis of Assisi wedded Dame Poverty, he was not following any different route, whatever his part in the Crusades. That is to say, in conclusion, that the humble engagement with life undertaken by L'Arche relates to history's most decisive conversions in the search for God. That being so, it is hardly surprising that L'Arche elicits this kind of response.

> He became Lord not on account of the sufferings of others but by his own sufferings. He was the first to taste bitterness. For he explained to us that one does not become his disciple by being called disciple, but by enduring the torments of discipleship in one's own heart.
>
> (St Ephrem the Syrian, *Commentary on the Diatesseron*).

L'ARCHE AND CONTEMPLATION

MARK SANTER

For Mark Santer, L'Arche belongs to the tradition of contemplative rather than active communities. L'Arche refuses just to do good; instead people learn to wait, forming habits of attention, of receiving from one another. 'Presence takes precedence over project'; here is the 'intensity of attention to the present moment'. Communication is not 'a matter of words only, but of body and spirit as a whole'. L'Arche is thus a 'school of attention to God'.

L'Arche is a community, or a community of communities, in which people of differing gifts and abilities live together. L'Arche is also deeply religious – and indeed Christian – in its primary inspiration. In Christian tradition it has been usual to categorise religious communities as either active or contemplative. In fact, there never was a truly Christian community, however devotedly given to good works, which did not have its contemplative dimension; nor ever a truly Christian community, however deeply given to prayer, whose members did not love and care for one another in practical ways.

Where does L'Arche belong on the active–contemplative spectrum? An outsider, who had simply heard about L'Arche as a kind of religious community caring for handicapped people, would naturally expect to categorise it as active rather than contemplative. And yet anyone who has ever experienced, however briefly, the life of L'Arche, will have found that they have entered a community which is profoundly contemplative in spirit. It is no accident that the experience of living for some months as members of L'Arche has led a number of young volunteers to recognise their calling to the contemplative life.

This contemplative spirit is not to be attributed simply to the presence of a church or an oratory among the facilities available to the community members – although it is true that the provision of a holy space at the heart of a community is very important for nurturing a spirit of prayer. Of more profound significance is the relationship between the prayers, wherever they are offered, and the quality of the life of the community as a whole. Here several aspects of the life of L'Arche are particularly significant to the contemplative spirit.

The value of waiting

In contrast with the spirit of contemplation, the active spirit likes to be in charge. It promotes a clear distinction between those who are doing good and those who are receiving it. It imposes itself, it organises, it sets goals and objectives, it likes to work by timetable. But to work in this way with the handicapped is to do violence to their dignity. It can be done only at the expense of their weakness.

This L'Arche refuses to do. Here, people have to learn to wait for each other, and to wait not for the clock but for the right time. Patience is central. The assistants are working and living with people who do not operate by contract, but who respond to attention, responding when they are ready to respond.

The habits of attention and waiting are habits of contemplation, in which we receive as well as give, in which we are acted upon as well as acting. In consequence, without in any way denying inherent differences of competence and responsibility, there is in such a setting no clear or simple line to be drawn between those who are active and those who are passive, between the doers and the receivers of good.

The value of the present moment

There are other things as well. L'Arche is a place where presence takes precedence over project. In living with people whose life is centred on the present, rather than on plans or projects for the day after tomorrow, the quality of the present moment is what matters above all. In such a life there is an intensity of attention to the present moment, which thereby takes on something of the quality of eternity. This too is of the essence of contemplation, as a kind of anticipation of the life of heaven, in which past and future are all contained in one eternal present.

The value of attention

Again, in a life centred on activity, the verbal is of primary importance. Things are verbalised and discussed. Plans are formed, orders are given, instructions are put into effect. When people are aggrieved with one another, they put their quarrels into words, and when they make things up, reconciliation is accompanied by discussion.

But in a place such as L'Arche, there is of necessity a manner and level of communication which transcends or goes deeper than the merely verbal. Communication in such a community is self-evidently a matter not of words only, but of body and spirit as a whole. This reveals another dimension in which L'Arche can function as a school of contemplation. Contemplative prayer is above all a matter of presence and attention. It cannot do without words, but it goes deeper than words.

There is an inseparability between attention to God and attention to other people. That ought not to be surprising – after all, attention is a form of love. So a school of attention to other people, such as L'Arche, is at the same time a school of attention to God. That is why, in a world scarred by activism, manipulation and godlessness, L'Arche is a place and source of healing.

In the following words, W. H. Auden was addressing a fellow poet. But he could equally have been speaking to a man or woman of prayer and contemplation:

In the deserts of the heart
Let the healing fountain start,
In the prison of his days
Teach the free man how to praise.

9

NORMALITY AND CONVERSION

NICHOLAS PETER HARVEY

The prophetic action of a person with considerable handicaps leads Peter Harvey to comment on a contradiction at the heart of L'Arche: communion without intercommunion for fear of straining relations with the Roman Catholic hierarchy. From this starting-point we are all challenged to respond as our own unconscious blind-spots are brought home to us.

As a result of a visit to L'Arche headquarters, I was sent a book telling the story of Nick Vereker, a considerably handicapped person who was part of a L'Arche community for many years. At that time the policy of L'Arche on eucharistic participation was that the rules of all the Churches must be observed. In consequence Nick, being an Anglican, was not allowed to receive communion at a Roman Catholic Mass. There could never be a communion service within his L'Arche home at which all could receive the sacrament. At the same time, the L'Arche ethos gave crucial significance to sacramental communion, members being encouraged to communicate in their own Churches. Frustrated, Nick took it upon himself to celebrate a simple form of communion in the house one night, distributing the elements to those present. This was done with great reverence.

The reaction of L'Arche staff was that, while the logic of this action was clear, it must not happen again. Implicit in this reservation was the view that Nick, because of his handicap, was not able fully to understand and appreciate the reason for the prohibition of intercommunion against which his behaviour was a protest.

It seems to me that Nick Vereker's action that night was prophetic, expressing a sure insight into a contradiction in the life of L'Arche which the leaders had perhaps not quite seen, or had not been able fully to address. There are always reasons in such matters – in this case, the view of the leadership that it was extremely important that relations between L'Arche and the Roman Catholic hierarchy should not become strained. I do not condemn that concern, nor is this written in order to criticise L'Arche. My suggestion is that the episode is an example of the extreme difficulty all humans have in transcending notions of what it is to be normal. The story has a peculiar poignancy precisely because L'Arche is so dedicated to living with and for the handicapped, and to learning in this way to recognise their humanity to the full. Yet in this matter of eucharistic policy, Nick was rendered powerless. He had a strongly held opinion, dramatically demonstrated in his action, that L'Arche's attitude to the Eucharist was self-contradictory. In practice he had no voice, being judged to be incompetent to have an opinion worthy of serious consideration.

I would defy anyone who feels at all smug about this story to claim that they are entirely free of comparable notions of human normality and abnormality. It is all very well to argue, in theory and in general, that all humans are just different from each other, that there is no norm and that the question of abnormality does not arise. It is always in the particular that our bluff is called, as we find difficulty in accommodating a person, or an aspect of a person, within our definition of the human. These attitudes are largely unconscious – innocent in that sense – and so inaccessible to conscious decision-making, unless and until there is a crisis which finds us out as racist, sexist, or whatever.

Notions of political correctness by no means do the job. While such notions may well lead to formally correct behaviour, they do not touch the heart or provoke further conversion. In an unpublished paper on racism, the theologian Sebastian Moore points out that it is by our feelings, and the inevitable revelation of these feelings, that our attitudes to other people are recognised. However hard we try to conceal our feelings of revulsion or discomfort in the presence of certain kinds of people, such feelings are writ large and will out.

These feelings reveal at once and indivisibly how we define humanity and how we understand God. I was once involved in a religious broadcast in which another contributor said, with obvious relish: 'God hates homosexuals. He loathes and detests them.' This man would of course have agreed with the Genesis claim that humans are made in God's image. In practice he was allowing his own unregenerate sense of the boundaries of the human to dictate his image of God as anti-homosexual.

Yet who can claim to hold consistently, and with heart-felt conviction in all circumstances, that the living God is a new way of understanding what it is to be human? Conversion is a process which takes a lifetime. It is the story of all our lives, incomplete until we die. It is so profound, so disturbing of the universe, that it *needs* a lifetime. We need not therefore be merely appalled by critical recognition of how incomplete the process is, in one or other respect, at any one moment. The human story is an adventure of becoming, and we cannot expect that to happen all at once. It is only a static morality of idealisation which would condemn out of hand the limitations of L'Arche's attitude to Nick Vereker. What matters more is whether we are ready to respond as and when our own unconscious blind-spots and antipathies are brought home to us. The sudden touch of grace, the uncovenanted glimpse of the transcendent, invites us to say yes to a further chapter in our own becoming.

10

THE SACRAMENTS IN L'ARCHE

A. M. (DONALD) ALLCHIN

Donald Allchin explores the sacramental life of L'Arche, focusing on bodiliness and brokenness. L'Arche helps us to face 'the daily reality of death', and so reflect on dying and rising in baptism, while finding the presence of Christ's 'life-giving death' in the Eucharist. The sacraments find new meaning in touch, in daily caring for bodies, washing and feeding. In L'Arche, the rite of foot-washing has acquired special importance because in this act, members of divided Churches, and even non-Christians, can share.

In any thought about the meaning and practice of the sacramental life in the context of the communities of L'Arche, two categories at once suggest themselves – bodiliness and brokenness. The lives of those with serious learning difficulties are lived very much at the level of the body, and frequently include painful experiences of brokenness – physical, psychological and social. In this way they open up special possibilities of approach to two of the basic ways in which the sacraments, and especially the sacrament of the Eucharist, have been understood throughout Christian history – that is to say, in terms of the presence and the sacrifice of the body of Christ. The way in which the presence and the sacrifice have been understood has, of course, been the source of long and bitter controversy, but no one who has maintained the practice of the sacraments has doubted that they are concerned, in one way or another, with discerning the body of Christ, and with entering into Christ's death and resurrection.

However, behind those two terms – bodiliness and brokenness –

there lies another, which is even more fundamental and which is strongly illuminated by the experience of L'Arche: this is humility. The sacraments reveal to us, in the most simple and immediate way, the immense humility of God who empties himself of his glory to come down to the level of our life in space and time, our life caught up in the knots of sin and death. This thought of the sacraments as making available to us the humility of God, revealed in the incarnation, is beautifully expressed by a theologian of the seventeenth century, Edward Reynolds, who, having conformed in the time of the Commonwealth, became Bishop of Norwich on the restoration of the episcopate in 1661.

Reynolds sees God's mercy in the sacraments as speaking directly to our senses, the babes in the human microcosm, leaving aside, at least for a time, the wise and prudent – our rational and spiritual faculties:

> Certainly, as the Son of God did admirably humble himself in his hypostatical union, unto a visible flesh, so doth he still, with equal wonder and lowliness, humble himself in a sacramental union unto visible elements. Strange it is, that that mercy which is so wonderful that the angels desire to look into it, so unconceivable, that it hath not entered into the thought of man; of such height and length and breadth and depth as passeth knowledge, should yet be made the object of our lowest faculties, and that which is hid from the wise and prudent in man's little world, his mind and spirit, should be revealed unto the babes, his senses ... So humble is his mercy, that since we cannot raise our understandings to the comprehension of divine mysteries, he will bring them down and submit those mysteries to the apprehension of our senses.[1]

What is true of the little world of the human person is no less true of the greater world of human society. In the social life of redeemed humanity which is Christ's Church, things are revealed to the babes which are hidden from the wise and prudent. It is one of the functions of L'Arche to reveal the reality hidden in this pious statement.

Entering the sacramental mystery

If the life of L'Arche opens up to us new possibilities of understanding the bodiliness and brokenness of human experience, the development of Christian reflection on the meaning of the Church's worship, in the last 50 years of the liturgical movement, has been constantly reminding us that behind the Latin word *sacramentum* there lies the Greek word *musterion*. All the Church's sacraments have their origin and meaning in the mystery which is Christ himself, *Christ the Sacrament of the Encounter with God* (1963), to cite the title of one of the earliest books of Edward Schillebeeckx.

It is Christ in his paschal mystery – that is to say, in the mystery of his passing over from death into life – who is actively present in all the sacraments. By sharing in those sacraments we come to share afresh in that passage through death into life, which becomes ours in him. One of the gifts of L'Arche is its capacity to help us to face the daily reality of death – a reality which our age and our society always tries to hide from us. The fragility of those who are seriously handicapped opens them, and us, to constant discoveries of limitation, frustration and mortality. 'We are familiar with death here', said Jean Vanier, speaking of the life of the community at Trosly. These words were taken up by a newcomer to L'Arche, when he spoke of finding at Trosly a place where it is possible 'to face death and handicap in a certain spirit which blends utter realism with hope and joy'.

The mystery of baptism

This realism of the constant facing of death in and through the death of Christ, helps us to reflect on the sacraments with new insight. We say that all the sacraments mean dying and rising with Christ – but we often underplay the aspect of brokenness and dying in our desire to be positive and affirmative about Christian faith. But the water of the font is not only the water of cleansing and new life; it is also the water in which an old order is destroyed so that a new order may be begun. The passage through the Red Sea involves destruction as well as liberation.

We say that in baptism we die with Christ and rise again with him, but our manner of celebrating the sacrament, by pouring a very small quantity of water on to the forehead of the person baptised, does not help us to realise the meaning of what we say. By contrast, a friend who was baptised in adult life, into the Orthodox Church, told me that at his baptism, the first time the priest pushed his head under the water – in the name of the Father – he thought, 'This is very interesting'; the second time – in the name of the Son – he thought, 'This must be what dying and rising with Christ means'; the third time – in the name of the Holy Spirit – his reaction was simply, '*Help!*'

If the baptism both of infants and of adults in our Western Churches were more normally done by total immersion, as it should be, we might begin to acquire a more living experience of the meaning of the sacrament. We might also begin to rediscover some of the other constituent elements in the rite as it was performed in the early Christian centuries. This too would give us a more bodily sense of its sacramentality.

Thomas Deacon, one of the later scholars of the eighteenth-century non-juring movement, in a catechism published in 1747, having explained that there are two great sacraments, goes on to ask:

Q. How many of the Lesser Sacraments are there?
A. Ten.
Q. Which are they?
A. Five belonging to Baptism, namely Exorcism, Anointing with Oil, the White Garment, a Taste of Milk and Honey, and Anointing with Chrism or Ointment.[2]

As we shall see, L'Arche's sense of the bodiliness of the human experience of God tends to extend the category of sacrament in something of this kind of way. Para-liturgies evolve which work out and embody the different elements of the central meaning of the rite.

The mystery of the Eucharist
If baptism is dying and rising with Christ, so in a still more profound way is the Eucharist. Though firmly rooted in the brokenness and

bodiliness of this world, the Eucharist is always opening up a way in and through this world into the world to come. It is not static, but full of movement through death into life. As Luther says: 'The sacrament is thus for us a bridge, a door, a ship, in which and through which we travel from this world into eternal life'. In our recent attempts to emphasise the corporate and social aspects of the Eucharist, we have perhaps tended to lose sight of this openness towards the last things which is implied in the breaking of the bread, which is also the breaking of the body in death – a breaking which in the mystery of Christ's Passover involves the destruction of death and the discovery of eternal life.

This awareness of the presence of the life-giving death of Christ in the sacrament of the Eucharist has two consequences which have particular importance in the context of L'Arche. First there is the sense that the Eucharist is celebrated with, and on behalf of, all, those who have died, no less than those who are still alive. For those of us whose Churches passed through the Reformation in the six-teenth century, this is an aspect of faith which we need to discover and experience anew.

A contemporary of Thomas Deacon, Thomas Rattray, Bishop of Edinburgh (d.1743), says, commenting on the writings of St Cyril of Jerusalem:

> And as for that expression in him, 'that God through their prayers and supplications would receive our petitions', he does not seem to have taken it from the liturgy but has added it only to show one great design of this commemoration, viz., that we may reap the benefit of their prayers and supplications for us; as he immediately after says that the dead are also greatly bene-fited by our prayers at the altar for them; and these two, viz., their prayers for us and ours for them are undoubtedly the two great branches of the communion of saints.[3]

Closely linked with this is the sense that in our union with Christ in his self-offering, his sufferings become ours and ours become his. To quote Thomas Rattray again:

As by this strict union betwixt him, the head and us the members, his sufferings are imputed to us, so ours also are imputed to him, so as not so much to be reckoned our own sufferings as the sufferings of Christ in us, and we are said to fill up what is wanting of the afflictions of Christ in our flesh, for his body's sake which is the Church.[4]

I suspect that at this point there is a co-inherence of human and divine, and of suffering and joy, which is known in L'Arche with a particular strength.

The presence of the Spirit

We have thought of the sacraments of baptism and Eucharist in terms of the presence of Christ's death and resurrection in the midst of his people and in the midst of his world. But the sacraments are not only the perpetual presence of Easter at the heart of the Church; they are also the perpetual presence of Pentecost. It is only in the power of the holy, good and life-giving Spirit that they become real, living mysteries of divine and human mercy and humility.

This is particularly the case in baptism, for the Spirit is given in baptism. But baptism is to be understood not as the washing in water alone, but as also including other rites such as the laying on of hands and the anointing with chrism. We need not, in this context, rehearse the controversies and uncertainties which surround the relation of baptism to confirmation. Perhaps it may be helpful to recall Thomas Deacon's *five* lesser sacraments linked with baptism. Perhaps it may also be helpful to recall that the anointing with oil is supposed to touch all our five senses, so that the whole body may be healed and transformed by the presence of the Holy Spirit, by the gifts of life which the Spirit gives.

Here again, in this anointing of the senses – of touch and taste, of hearing and seeing and feeling, which is their sealing by the Holy Spirit – we have great possibilities of rediscovering the bodiliness of the sacraments and their aptitude for healing. Here, the experience of L'Arche, in bathing and touching the bodies of those most severely handicapped, is full of suggestion. There is a healing power in touch, in anointing, in the use of scented oils, which we need to explore further.

When we come to the Eucharist, the presence of the Spirit can be realised in many ways. One which is underlined in the context of L'Arche is the gathering together of the Church into unity, in and through its immense diversity. We are such different people, we have such different gifts and such different experiences. We learn here that they can come together into one in the life of the Spirit who diversifies at the same time as she unifies.

Another aspect of the action of the Spirit in the Eucharist, which the experience of L'Arche can help us to appreciate, is the aspect of joy – yes, it may be of ecstatic joy. For me this thought is inevitably linked with my very first meeting with L'Arche, in the solemn Eucharist of Easter Day in Canterbury Cathedral in 1974 – an occasion on which the healing power of spontaneity and joy was released within the structures of an elaborate and formal act of worship, bringing about a remarkable wholeness, a joyful solemnity.

Here the restoration of the bodily nature of the Eucharist, in that all are invited to receive from the chalice, is of great significance. If the bread is the broken body which is given for the life of the world, the wine is not only the blood poured out, it is the wine of the kingdom, the joy at the fulfilment of all things, which we taste already here and now. Here the Churches which have passed through the sixteenth-century Reformation have something to give to the Christian family as a whole. I think of the more ecstatic of Charles Wesley's eucharistic hymns, and of some of the sermons of Lancelot Andrewes and N.F.S. Grundtvig. Both insist that in drinking from the chalice we are drinking from the one Spirit, and that our spirits are already touched and changed by the joy of an eternal feast in which God shall be all and in all.

The sacraments of daily life

We have been looking at some aspects of the meaning of the sacraments of baptism and Eucharist, as they bring us into the mystery of Christ's dying and rising through the coming of the Spirit. We turn now to look at those same sacraments from a more human and empirical perspective – to consider them anthropologically as well as theologically.

The first point is very simple, yet at the same time all-embracing. Baptism and Eucharist are rooted in two actions which are a necessary part of human life from birth to death: the infant needs to be washed and fed every day; and often, at the end of life, we are again in need of having these things done for us.

These actions are vital for our personal existence; they are also vital for our social existence. Eating together is one of the primary ways of creating human community. Some anthropologists suggest that the human habit of washing daily (grooming) is a necessary part of our making ourselves socially and sexually acceptable.

It is clear that L'Arche has a particular experience of these basic human actions. Washing and cleaning those who cannot perform these functions for themselves are a basic part of daily life in the communities. As Jean Vanier constantly stresses, washing the body when it is broken or in pain is an essential way of caring for the person, and an essential way of expressing and communicating love ('Touch is a primal form of communication').

We have seen how, in its earlier history, the Church associated anointing with washing. The body was plunged into water, then all the senses were anointed. Here are forms of sacramental action which may be realised in various ways in communities where washing plays so central a part.

Eating together is also at the very heart of a L'Arche community. Here there is a distinction to be made which may be of some importance. Some have to be fed individually – infants, the very old when they are extremely weak, the most severely handicapped; others are able to sit at table together. Both these ways of eating need to be respected and valued. Both need to be present in our celebration of the sacrament.

When we eat together and talk together at the same time, there is a particular way of linking body, mind and spirit – or, in theological terms, uniting word and sacrament. As a contemporary poet puts it, in a poem called *Having Our Tea*:

Stupid, they say, to think of the thing as an ordinance.
And yet all the elements are found to change in our hands.
Because we sit and share them with each other
There's a miracle. There's a binding of unmerited graces
By the cheese, and through the apples and the milk,
A new creation of life is established, a true presence.
And talking to each other, breaking words over food
Is somehow different from customary chatting . . .
Still tea is not worship. But it overcomes
Things so the Spirit may happily hop
In our hearts. Assimilating heaven's carol
Into our constitutions, we are a choir, our throats
Blending calories and words together in the presence
Of the unseen Conductor who laid the table.[5]

This is something which is common to all human societies which
have maintained the custom of sharing meals and talking over them.
All through the Gospels we hear of shared meals, and Jesus constantly uses parables of shared meals. There are words and actions
here which all Christians remember, and which are part of the foundation of the life of L'Arche.

Service – a sacramental sign

It is not surprising that the L'Arche communities should have
found themselves experiencing the sacraments in new ways, and
experimenting with new ways of celebrating the sacraments. These
experiments are in part due to the demands made on communities
which gather together Christians of separate Churches not in communion with one another, and which more widely gather together
people belonging to totally different religious traditions (e.g. Hindu,
Muslim or Buddhist). Here is a particular experience of the brokenness of human society which needs to be taken up into a context of
healing.

But it is not only these ecumenical problems which lead to new
ways of celebrating the sacraments. Quite apart from them, it has

been necessary to find ways of celebrating which take more account of our bodiliness and brokenness than has been usual in our liturgical practice for a long time.

Here, without doubt, the most striking, and in some ways most important, example of sacramental exploration has been the rediscovery of the rite of foot-washing. Seeing the importance of washing the body in the life of the communities, it is not surprising that this particular action of Jesus' has spoken insistently in the L'Arche context. Rites of foot-washing are used in different situations, sometimes private and domestic, sometimes public and ecclesiastical – as when the two bishops of Cork, Roman Catholic and Church of Ireland, washed one another's feet in the context of a L'Arche Holy Week celebration.

In the life of L'Arche itself, the rite of foot-washing has acquired a special importance when people from divided Churches (or from different religions) announce the covenant together. As the practice of announcing the covenant developed and became established, it became clear that it was not possible to do it in the context of the Eucharist if all those taking part could not participate fully. After much reflection it was suggested that the covenant should be announced in the context of an act of worship which found its climax in the act of washing of feet.

There was nothing arbitrary in this proposal. The fact that in the Fourth Gospel the narrative of the feet-washing takes the place of the narrative of the Last Supper suggested insistently that this was a possible way through an apparently impossible situation. So it has proved to be. The rite which has been devised is given on pp. 112–18. The long eucharistic prayer at its heart attempts to summarise its meaning and intention.

Another sacramental sign, which has developed in the context of the divided Eucharist, is that of receiving a blessing from the celebrant at the moment when it is not possible to receive the sacrament itself. Thérèse Vanier and Maggie Smith have written about this practice with sensitivity and understanding. The practice of L'Arche in this matter undoubtedly played some part in encouraging the much more public use of this sign at the services which inaugurated the new Council of Churches of Britain and Ireland.

At a less public level, the communities themselves tend to develop a variety of para-liturgies at high points in the Church's year, particularly at Christmas, in Holy Week and at Easter. Such rites are also an important part of many domestic occasions – the celebration of anniversaries, birthdays, partings and reunions. The bodiliness and the brokenness enter into such occasions, which underline the vital human dimensions of *anamnesis*, celebration and thanksgiving. We discover who we are in remembering and giving thanks.

Perhaps above all, the para-liturgies of L'Arche help us to remember not only our bodiliness and brokenness but also the provisionality of our life in time. This represents the provisional character of a Church which has rediscovered itself as a pilgrim people on the way to the kingdom. In that pilgrimage there are moments of joy and celebration, when the end of the journey is suddenly already given to us, realised in anticipation here and now. Such moments, which involve re-calling and expectation, help to restore to us the fullness of experience of life in a world of space and time. This is an experience which has place for haste and anticipation, for patience and perseverance, and for the contemplative realisation of the eternal goal made known already in our midst.

As Ann Griffiths put it, in a memorable verse:

> I shall walk slowly all my days
> Under the shadow of the blood of the cross,
> And as I walk I shall run,
> And as I run I shall stand still
> And see the salvation which shall be mine
> When I come to rest in the grave.

Para-liturgy of washing of the feet (1988)

Assemble in bare feet, at far end of the chapel.

Celebrant   Now before the hour of the Passover, when Jesus knew that his hour had come to depart out of this world to the Father, having loved his own who were in the world, he loved them to the end. (John 13:1)

Sing   **Veni Sancte Spiritus**

Two people carry in the Bible which is placed on the altar. All follow to form a semicircle at the front of the chapel, standing.

Celebrant   Welcome.

Confession

All   **Almighty God, our heavenly Father, we have sinned against you and against our fellow men and women, in thought and word and deed, through negligence, through weakness, through our own deliberate fault. We are truly sorry and repent of all our sins.**

For the sake of your Son Jesus Christ, who died for us, forgive us all that is past; and grant that we may serve you in newness of life to the glory of your name. Amen.

Sing   **Lord have mercy**

Gloria

All then sit in groups for readings.

Old Testament reading: Isaiah 58:6–12

Psalm (sung with responses)

Epistle: Philippians 2:5–11

All   **Alleluia.**

Stand

Celebrant 'Do you understand', he said, 'what I have done to you? You call me Master and Lord, and rightly so; so I am. If I then, the Lord and Master, have washed your feet, you should wash each other's feet. I have given you an example so that you may copy what I have done to you.' (John 13:12–15)

All   **Alleluia.**

Gospel: John 13:1–17

Homily

All move forward into semicircle.

Renewal of baptismal vows

Celebrant In our baptism we died with Christ and were buried with him so that we might rise with him to a new life within the family of his Church. Today we renew the promises made at our baptism, affirm our allegiance to Christ, and our rejection of all that is evil.

Therefore I ask these questions:
Do you turn to Christ?

All   **I turn to Christ.**

Celebrant Do you repent of your sins?

All   **I repent of my sins.**

Celebrant Do you renounce evil?

All   **I renounce evil.**

Celebrant And now I ask you to make the profession of Christian faith into which you were baptised, and in which you live and grow.

Do you believe and trust in God the Father, who made the world?

All	**I believe in God, the Father almighty, creator of heaven and earth.**
Celebrant	Do you believe and trust in his Son Jesus Christ, who redeemed mankind?
All	**I believe in Jesus Christ, his only Son our Lord, he was conceived by the power of the Holy Spirit and born of the Virgin Mary. He suffered under Pontius Pilate, was crucified, died and was buried, he descended to the dead. On the third day he rose again. He ascended into heaven, and is seated at the right hand of the Father. He will come again to judge the living and the dead.**
Celebrant	Do you believe and trust in his Holy Spirit, who gives life to the people of God?
All	**I believe in the Holy Spirit, the holy Catholic Church, the communion of saints, the forgiveness of sins, the resurrection of the body, and life ever-lasting. Amen.**
Celebrant	This is the faith of the Church.
All	**This is our faith. We believe and trust in one God. Father, Son and Holy Spirit.**

Song

Announcing the covenant

The priests of the different denominations who receive the Covenant call out the names of those announcing the Covenant.
Each in turn comes forward to the priest of his/her own tradition in the language of the person concerned.

Celebrant	... (name) you are invited to live a Covenant at L'Arche with Jesus and with all your brothers and sisters, especially the poorest and the weakest. Do you want this?

(A couple who belong to different denominations will be asked the question by both priests together.)
When all who are announcing the Covenant have done so, everyone returns to their group places.

Prayer before the washing of the feet

Celebrant   Father,
all-powerful and ever-living God,
we do well always and everywhere to give you thanks,
through Jesus Christ our Lord.
You sent your Son to live among us,
so that we might learn from him humility and obedience.
His nature was divine,
yet he did not cling to his equality with God,
but emptied himself
to assume the condition of a slave.
He became as we are,
and was humbler yet,
accepting death, even death on a cross.
But you, Father, raised him high,
and gave him a name which is above all names,
so that we can acclaim
JESUS IS LORD
to your honour and glory,
and join with the whole company of heaven and earth,
saying:
    Holy, Holy, Holy Lord,
    God of power and might
    heaven and earth are full of your glory.
    Hosanna in the highest.
    Blessed is he who comes in the name of the Lord.
    Hosanna in the highest.

Father,
we thank you for the great gift of Jesus your Son,
for the example he gave us of love and service,

for his promise to be with those who love and follow
him.

Having loved his own, he loved them to the end.
On the night before he gave his life for us,
knowing that the Father had put everything into his
hands
Jesus met with his disciples
and gave them his new commandment:
      'Love one another as I have loved you.'

Getting up from table,
He took a towel and water,
washed his disciples' feet,
and said:
            'I have given you an example.
            You are to do for one another
            what I have done for you.'

As we remember Jesus,
his life,
his love even unto death,
his resurrection,
we rejoice that he has given us his Spirit,
to be his hands and body now in the world.

We ask the Holy Spirit to create in us
the mind that was in Christ Jesus,
to enable us to live and love as he did,
without counting the cost;
without losing heart.

May the Holy Spirit reveal to us
always more fully
the presence of Jesus in the poorest and the weakest.
May we listen to them,
receive their gifts,
and be led into a healing covenant with them.

We remember those in the past,
people revered by the Church,
people we have known,
who have given us an example
of what the love of Jesus means.

Father,
we know ourselves to be weak and vulnerable,
we too are poor,
but it is in our poverty and brokenness
that you come to us,
and reveal the depths of your love.

For all this
we give you thanks
through Jesus Christ your Son
who lives and reigns with you
and the Holy Spirit
one God
for ever and ever.
Amen.

Then celebrants join a group themselves.

Washing the feet then takes place in silence.

Group leaders begin, going round the semicircle, each washing his neighbour's feet. The one who has received this then places his hand on the head of the person who has washed his feet, and prays silently with them. Each time after washing and drying feet, the bowl, jug and towel are replaced in the middle of group, where they are taken up by the next person after a brief pause.

After all have done this, a song is sung.

During the song the group leaders take up jugs and towels to the altar and place them in circle round it. All follow and form a semicircle around the altar.

Intercessions

All   **Our Father . . .**

Celebrant   May the Lord God bless you and keep you.
             May the Lord God let his face shine on you and be
             gracious to you.
             May the Lord God uncover his face to you and bring
             you peace.

             The peace

After the peace, song and dancing to the dining-room for celebration!

❧ Part III ❧

Sharers and carers think theologically

❧ 11 ❧

MAKING THE BODY WHOLE: SOME QUESTIONS ABOUT SCRIPTURE AND IMPAIRMENT

SIMON HORNE

The driver of a minibus hired to transport a group of children with mental and physical disabilities said to the person accompanying them, 'What on earth have the parents done to have children like this?' Such reactions may remind us of certain passages in the Bible. People who have disabilities often report that there are Christians who confront them with the Bible, and suggest that if they had enough faith they would be healed. This makes them feel unacceptable and guilty. Such negative experiences are the starting-point for Simon Horne's exploration of Scripture. By reading the Bible in its ancient context, he provides a different perspective. For him, people's attitudes are a major contributing factor in making those who happen to have defective bodily functions (or impairments) into people who are disabled by social and physical barriers. His study of the Bible shows how we need the presence of impaired people, and how they embody discipleship qualities.

In both Testaments of Scripture, there are many passages of impairment[1] – stories about people with impairments, and diverse uses of impairment images. Textual and archaeological evidence from the cultures in which the books of Scripture were compiled show that people with impairments were common, and also that they were present, often in active ways, at all levels of society. When using impairment to communicate their experience of God, the writers of Scripture spoke what they saw, and what they knew. To understand the impairment texts of Scripture, glimpses of the cultural backgrounds of these texts are required. In Western cultures, where people with impairments are not present in an active way at all levels of society, so much of the content of scriptural impairment texts is strange and obscure to us. The experience of people who live impairment today will release the riches of those texts.

Modernity brought the enlightening message that humankind could remove the infirmities of the world by Progress, and the Industrial Revolution sanctified efficiency and productiveness. As a result, the impairment that could not be removed by medical science was removed into institutions. And those people whose physical or mental condition impeded their productivity evolved into the passive objects of efficient protection. People with impairments became unseen and unknown. To a large extent, this is still how things are today: impaired people are far from active at all levels of society; they are little more than occasionally seen, and they are not known.[2] So for us to hear the living word of God, which the writers of Scripture were communicating using familiar aspects of impairment, we must know something of the experience of people who live impairment today. Their experience will unlock expressions of God's word that have become unfamiliar to us.

But people who live impairment today are not being encouraged to relate their experience to Scripture. On the contrary, Scripture is frequently used as a weapon against people with impairments: they are told that their impairments (and so they themselves) are unacceptable to God; they are handicapped with guilt – if they only had enough faith, they are told, God would take their impairment away. What they know from their experience to be true – that they are not simply victims, objects of charity, but that they have distinctive contributions to make to society – this is denied. In each of these examples, Scripture is the chief weapon brandished against people with impairments.

So, far from being encouraged to relate their experience to Scripture, people with impairments are being driven away from the Church – an act which is self-destructive, for they are vital. When people with impairments are cut off, Christ's body is mutilated. Without people who live impairment listening to and interpreting the living song of God in Scripture, our hearing of God's word is impaired.

To those living impairment, we say, 'It is to the shame of Christ's body that Scripture has been used abusively as a cudgel against you. For the texts of Scripture themselves tell us: your impairment is not unacceptable to God; the removal of your impairment is not required by God, let alone prevented by your alleged lack of faith; your presence and distinctive participation in society is a requirement. Without you, as people with impairments, Christ's body cannot be made whole, and without your experience as the focus, our hearing of God's living word being sung to us all through Scripture is disabled.'

Glimpses of impairment in ancient times

Trauma, accidental and inflicted, was one of the most common causes of injury and disability, and is one of the most frequent causes of pathological conditions apparent in ancient skeletal remains . . . A variety of states of disability must have existed anciently, owing to many causes.

(*Anchor Bible Dictionary*, vol. V, p. 67)

Archaeological remains and written texts from the cultures in which the Scriptures were compiled show that people with impairments participated at all levels of society. We see this in evidence from paleopathologists' analyses of human remains, from surviving prostheses (including adapted boots, artificial limbs and eyes), and from representations in carvings, inscriptions, paintings and vases.[3] The richest source for our understanding of how things were for people with impairments is written material, especially Graeco-Roman texts. Impairment emerges across a full spectrum of genres: from philosophy and histories, to satirical epigrams and tragedy, from botany, art history, and writings about the gods, to phonetics, love-poetry and astrology.

People were interested in impairment; it was a topic for both popular and specialist writers. There are entertaining personal

descriptions in narrative: of the emperor Claudius and King Agesi-
laus of Sparta; the aristocrat Domitius Tullus; Battus the explorer,
who founded the Greek colony in Libya; politicians such as Demos-
thenes and Lycurgus; philosophers, painters, poets and musicians –
including both Aesop and Homer; beggars, priests, artisans, slaves,
entertainers and lovers; parents and children; thieves and practical
jokers; veterans and serving soldiers, including Philoctetes (without
whom the Greeks could not capture Troy) and Hannibal; the seers
Teiresias (who saw through Oedipus) and Phineus (guide to Jason
and the Argonauts); the Cyclops Polyphemus, son of Neptune, who
was blinded by Odysseus. Even deities are included: Hephaestus,
whose skill 'not any of the gods is able to withstand'; Horus / Harpo-
crates, the son of Isis and Osiris; Plutus the god of wealth, and the
Litae, the prayers, the healing daughters of Zeus. Ancient interest in
impairment is also seen from the detailed classification in medical
treatises, on spinal injuries in Egyptian material; limb-fractures and
eye diseases in Mesopotamian texts; paralysis, spinal curvature,
speech and hearing loss in the Greek writings; or in the Syrian *Book
of Medicines*, impairment from damage to the brain.

Impairment was also much used as imagery – for example, in the
terms used to describe silent vowels, a blunted instrument, obtuse
angles; a setting sun or waning moon; the numbing effect of frost
and narcotics; the sounds made by children and birds; dressed trees
and grafted plants; irregular metres in verse. Philosophers liked to
use impairment imagery to describe people unable or unwilling to see
the truth. The inability of impairment is turned to entertaining
paradox with, for example, statues of great orators that cannot speak,
or the mute messenger – a fire beacon. The suddenness of a stroke
describes astonishment and interruption. The loosening of a limb in
paralysis is applied to relaxation, and the cancelling of debt or marriage. In an early Jewish tradition, the complementary fitting
together of body and soul after death is described by means of a story
of one person who is unable to see, and another who is unable to
walk, each helping the other to thwart their able-bodied neighbours.
In Egyptian and Babylonian texts, impairment is used to illustrate
sudden or striking reversals of fortune. People in the ancient world

were familiar with impairment. Ancient writers made full use of what they saw.

The Lord gives and the Lord takes away

I want to explore two impairment themes from the ancient world, alongside a number of passages from Scripture. The two themes are that impairment comes from the gods, and that impairment is taken away by the gods. Among other scriptural passages, we will look at the Leviticus verses in which the impaired priest is said to be unacceptable and may not draw near, and at some of Jesus' healings of impairment. Impaired people identify these passages in particular as ones most often wielded against them to say that they are unacceptable to God, that they are to blame for their impairment, that God requires their impairment be removed, and that there is no need for their distinctive participation in society.[4] With these two impairment themes from the ancient world we will see that the impairment texts of Scripture do not drive away people with impairments. On the contrary, the texts themselves show us how much impaired people are required in order that our understanding of the texts may be set free from its confinement.

In recent surveys of ancient medicine, scholars point out that medication, prayers, medical instruments and liturgy were used in complementary and co-operative ways in the diagnosis and treatment of infirmity. The religious dimension to healing was expressed differently across cultures, and articulated to a greater or lesser extent within them; but the role of the gods in causing and removing infirmity is expressed both in medical texts, and also in more general works. Although no clear distinction seems to have been made between illness and impairment, in surviving Egyptian and Greek medical treatises a distinction was made between curable and incurable conditions (among incurable conditions were included many impairments). In more general texts, impairments were also described as beyond human healing.

Many reasons were put forward for the gods' giving of impairment – punishment being by no means the predominant one: 'Most illnesses were not viewed as divine punishment'.[5] It was also recognised that, although human ability to effect cure for infirmity was inspired and guided by healing divinities, human healing had its limits: there were many incurable conditions, and impairments fall largely into this group. Occasionally these impossible healings do occur. When they do, the will and the power of the gods are clearly at work.

In what follows, we shall confine ourselves to studying the role of God in the Jewish–Christian tradition.

Giving impairment

With the present widespread interest in healing, God's hand in the bringing and taking away of infirmity is thoroughly documented across both Testaments by scholars of different traditions. For our purpose, we will focus specifically on impairment. God tells Moses that he is responsible for making a person impaired: ' "Who gives speech to mortals? Who makes them mute or deaf, seeing or blind? Is it not I, the Lord?" ' (Exod. 4:11). This is God's response to Moses' refusal to speak to the elders of Israel and to Pharaoh because of his speech impairment. God's anger is kindled against Moses for asking God to send someone else (Exod. 4:13), but there is no sense here of God giving impairment as a punishment – quite the reverse: God's statement makes it clear to Moses that God will be using him through his inability. Commentators explain that God chose Moses precisely because he had a speech impairment, 'in order that people might not say that it was his eloquence which convinced Israel'.[6]

In a similar way, Paul boasts of his own impairment, his own inability: 'that the power of Christ may rest upon me . . . I am content with inabilities . . . for when I am unable, then I have ability' (2 Cor. 12:9f). There are three dimensions in these verses. First, as with Moses, God reveals his power through Paul's patent inability. Compare 2 Corinthians 4:7: 'We have this treasure in earthen vessels, to show that the transcendent power belongs to God and not to us' (RSV). Secondly, by verbal allusion to the Greek Old Testament, Paul links Christ's coming to the presence of God in the tabernacle: Paul's inability is a holy place, the place of meeting Christ, as God was met in the tent of meeting. Thirdly, God tells Paul directly in a vision something quite extraordinary: 'My power is made complete in inability' (2 Cor. 12:9). Somehow, God's power is fulfilled, made whole, in inability. This is a paradox about God that Paul expresses elsewhere, of the emptying of Christ's ability on the cross: 'He was crucified in inability' (2 Cor. 13:4).[7]

As God's power was made complete in Christ's body crucified in inability, so God has made Christ's body, the Church, to be held together by inability (1 Cor. 12:18–25). Paul uses precise language to identify people who are less able as chosen, and intended by God for the specific task of holding the body of Christ together through mutual interdependence (1 Cor. 12:25); only people who are less able have the ability to do this, and for this reason God gives them extra honour (1 Cor. 12:22, 24). Christ's physical body was broken in inability; Christ's body the Church is held together by inability – and Paul goes even further, saying that God has inability (1 Cor. 1:25) (though this inability of God is more able than the abilities of humankind). Commentators and theologians do not do justice to this startling image: inability, according to Paul, is an aspect of God's nature.

In these passages relating to God's giving of impairment and working through inability, five questions arise: how is it that when people are unable, it is then that they have ability? How does Christ's power come to rest in human inability? How is it that God's power is made complete in inability? How can people who are less able hold the body of Christ together through mutual interdependence? How does God have inability? Whatever answers emerge, they will further illuminate the variety of reasons to be found in Scripture for God's giving of impairment: inability is the place where humankind has ability, it is where Christ's power comes to rest, it is the place where God's power is made complete, it is how the body of Christ is held together, it is an image of God's own nature.

What about sin?

The reason Jesus gives for someone having been born blind is: ' "So that God's working might be made known through him" ' (John 9:3). Jesus makes this statement to contradict his disciples, who show their lack of understanding by linking the man's impairment to sin, just as he contradicts a similar supposed link at Luke 13:2–5. Blindness is mentioned in the general list of infirmities with which God will smite his people for disobedience – although it is the effect of being blind that is stressed, not the blindness itself: 'You shall grope at noonday, as the blind grope in darkness' (Deut. 28:29 RSV). Similarly elsewhere, the effect of being blind, rather than blindness itself, is a punishment for those who practise injustice.[8] There are occasions when God makes people blind, but he does so temporarily, and for specific purposes: the men of Sodom are prevented from seizing the heavenly messengers (Gen. 19:11); the Arameans are prevented from seeing where Elisha leads them (2 Kings 6:18). So too Zechariah, in Luke 1:20, is made temporarily dumb. In a review of impairment texts of the Hebrew Bible, Jewish scholars state, 'Blindness in general is nowhere stated to be a punishment for sin'.[9]

The disciples' question to Jesus about the blind man demonstrates that there was a belief at that time that impairment was given as punishment. But this belief is by no means predominant in the New Testament. At three healing encounters, impairment and sin are set together. In one, Jesus denies the link (John 9:3). In another, Jesus explicitly says that he is healing the man to prove that he has the authority to forgive sin – not because the man's sin has caused his impairment or prevented his healing (Mark 2:3–12). In the other, Jesus tells the healed person to sin no more (John 5:14); if Jesus is here linking the person's impairment and sin, it is an instance both unique, and also contradictory to what the same Gospel writer quotes Jesus as saying four chapters later. Jesus' statement could be simply recognising that this person, like anyone else, committed sins. As in Luke 13:3,5, he could also be saying that whatever false links people may make between their behaviour and what happens to them, they are vulnerable to even worse punishment if they fail to repent.

A tradition in ancient thought, which also emerges in Scripture, saw punishment for sin as a cause of infirmity. As we have seen, this was one of many conjectured causes; in this again, Scripture reflects the texts of other ancient societies. There is little in Scripture specifically relating impairment and sin; many other reasons for the giving of impairment are identified, and some are developed theologically (e.g. by Paul in his letters).

Drawing near

Among passages from Scripture cited in support of impairment being unacceptable to God, are the lists of priests who 'may not draw near the altar', and of impaired sacrifices that 'will not be accepted' (Lev. 21:16–23, 22:20–25). The list of conditions making it unacceptable for priests to serve at the altar includes some which are common among today's clergy: fractures, short and long sight, arthritis – even baldness, according to the rabbinic reading of the verses! However, this passage also states that while men with impairments may not perform priestly duties, they are not prevented from enjoying the benefits of priesthood: 'He may eat the bread of his God, both of the most holy and of the holy' (Lev. 21:22), nor does the impaired priest lose his relationship with God: God is no less 'his God' (Lev. 21:17, 21, 22). Whatever the complexities of the priestly and purity systems in the Temple, even the Leviticus passage shows that impairment was not in itself unacceptable to God.

The ritual dimension to impairment in the Leviticus tradition is paradoxically reversed in other scriptural passages. The sacrifice acceptable to God is said to be an impaired heart: 'The sacrifice acceptable to God is a maimed spirit, a maimed and crushed heart' (Ps. 51:16f). Also, the impaired heart is where God is said to abide: 'I dwell on high, in holiness; and also with those whose hearts are crushed and maimed' (Isa. 57:15). New Testament writers too refer to the Leviticus tradition, saying that Christ alone was unblemished and unimpaired, as both sacrifice and priest; through his actions, all people can now draw near to the holy place.[10]

According to rabbinic readings of Leviticus, the restriction on performing priestly duties was originally given to prevent worshippers from being distracted by the priest's impairment; once the impairment had become familiar to worshippers, the restriction on the impaired priest could be lifted. Compare too the story in Jewish tradition of the archangel Michael complaining about the impaired Jacob acting as priest: God replies by affirming Jacob as his priest despite his impairment, 'Thou art my priest in heaven, and he is my priest on earth'. When Zechariah the priest becomes impaired while serving at the altar, the worshippers are not shocked at his impurity, nor do they fear that he is being punished – they assume he has experienced a vision. And despite his impairment, he continues to carry out his priestly duties (Luke 1:22f).

The Leviticus passage itself, as well as scriptural and extra-scriptural uses of the Leviticus tradition, show that impairment was not seen as being unacceptable to God – far from it, impairment in heart is both what God requires, and also where God abides. Other questions emerge: how is a maimed heart what God requires? What did the writers mean by saying that what impaired people experience in their bodies is what God requires of us all in our hearts? And how do we meet God in such a place?

Taking impairment away

Jesus' healings are often quoted at people with impairments to show their unacceptability to God. In Jesus, the argument goes, God's will was fulfilled; by taking away impairment, Jesus showed that impairment is not in God's will. We have already seen that Scripture shows impairment not as contrary to God's will, but as God-given. We can also apply the second of our impairment themes from ancient texts: beyond the ability of human healers, the taking away of impairment could only occur by divine power and will. Jesus several times heals impairment at a moment of controversy: forgiving sins, working on the Sabbath, allegedly using the power of Beelzebul.[11] In these controversies, Jesus' healing of impairment, his doing of the impossible, is used to prove that he has the authority to do and say what he does. This is shown in what Jesus says, and in the reaction of the crowd: ' "So that you may know that the Son of Man has authority on earth to forgive sins" . . . The crowd glorified God who had given such authority to human beings' (Matt. 9:6–8). The crowd focuses on Jesus' authority to forgive sins, not his healing of impairment. In the impossible impairment healings, Jesus demonstrates that what he controversially says and does is in the power and will of God.

In a number of healings, the faith of the impaired person is also a focus. This leads to people with impairments today being told that it is their lack of faith which prevents the removal of their impairment. But people in the narrative, identified by Jesus as having saving faith, are not blocking God's will in what they say or do; on the contrary, they embody discipleship qualities – and do so as impaired people. An example is Bartimaeus, a blind man at Jericho. In contrast to the crowd, he is persistent, and his persistence brings him to Jesus' attention. After receiving what he has asked for, Bartimaeus 'followed him on the way' – a phrase that brings out his representative role. Persistence is a theme of two of Jesus' discipleship parables (Luke 11:5–13; 18:1–8). Bartimaeus acts out in the narrative what Jesus teaches elsewhere in parables. In his commentary on Matthew's version of this story, John Chrysostom identifies people with impairments as models: 'Let us then emulate them!' (*Homilies on Matthew*, 66). Here, another question arises: the Gospel characters who model these discipleship qualities do so from their experience of impairment (Bartimaeus is explicitly contrasted with the crowd): what, in the experience of impaired people today, embodies these qualities?

Conclusion

We have explored two themes, identified from ancient literature, within scriptural impairment texts: God gives impairment, and God takes impairment away. Passages relating to God's working through impairment provoke a number of questions about God's giving of impairment. Impairment as punishment for sin is seen to have been a belief in Scripture, but a modest one, and one denied by Jesus. The Leviticus tradition, which keeps impaired priests and sacrifices from the altar, does not suggest that impairment in itself is unacceptable to God. Elsewhere in Scripture this tradition is reversed, and impairment is used to describe what God requires and what Christ has achieved. In New Testament healings, the fact that impairment is taken away is significant for the authority of Jesus' teaching. Impaired people in the narrative similarly reinforce his teaching by embodying discipleship qualities.

The impairment texts in Scripture were written in and for societies where impaired people were seen and known. These scriptural texts are vital to us, they are given to us as insights into the essentials of faith-full living and worship – insights as to the place of human ability, and where God's ability is made complete; how the body of Christ is held together; they offer a glimpse of God's nature; of where God dwells, and where the power of Christ comes to rest; of what God requires of us in our hearts; of how qualities of faith are embodied. When we consider people with impairment in the light of Scripture, riches are unlocked and fragrance broken open. This must happen in order that people amputated from the body can be incorporated into it. This is a requirement for the unimpeded hearing of God's song to us all. This is indispensable for the making whole of Christ's body.

✺ 12 ✺

BEING HUMAN

JOHN GOLDINGAY

John Goldingay explores what it means for humanity to be made in God's image. He suggests that the disabled have the capacity to reveal aspects of humanity which have been suppressed, especially by modernity. He explores this in relation first to the task God gave to humankind; second, to the concept of life as a journey in which we become what we are; third, to our need for relationships and for worship in which humanity is represented in its fullness and God is imaged; and fourth, to our bodiliness – we were not designed for self-sufficiency, and human life is corporate. 'Communities without disabled people are disabled communities.'

When people meet the disabled, sometimes their instinctive way of relating suggests that they subconsciously regard the disabled as not quite the same sort of beings as the rest of us. This applies to the physically disabled, but especially to those who are in some way disabled in spirit or mind. Our starting-point here is the conviction and the experience that when, as an 'ordinary' person, I meet someone who is disabled, I meet a person who is different from me in an important way, but who is a genuinely human being. There are analogies with what can happen when I meet someone of a different race. I meet someone else made in God's image. Their differentness contributes to my understanding of what it means to be human, and what it means to be God.

It is an aspect of the glory and the challenge of humanity that we are different from each other. If the diversity within humanity reflects our being made in God's image, it reflects the diversity within God which is epitomised in God's being Father, Son, and

Holy Spirit. Disabled people contribute to that diversity of humanity, modelling other ways of being human than the way of the abled. It is thus when abled and disabled live, work and worship together that humanity is represented in its fullness and God is imaged.

The statement that human beings were created in God's image has had a prominent place in discussion of what it means to be human, but it has functioned more as a vehicle upon which to project convictions, or as a stimulus to reflection, than as an explicit indicator of what it means to be human. Over the centuries the statement has thus rung a series of different bells. In ages which wanted to stress rationality, or morality, or humanity's spiritual nature, these each became that in which the image of God lay. Our age is inclined to stress creativity rather than conformity; relationship rather than inner being; body as well as spirit. Theological attention has thus been attracted to the fact that the image in which humanity was created is above all that of a creator; that the beings created in God's image are physical beings; and that Genesis goes on to tell us, 'God created humanity in God's own image, created it in the image of God, created it male and female' (Gen. 1:27, my translation).

Like much of Genesis 1–3 the notion of being in God's image has been able to stimulate or reflect so much theological thinking because it is a symbolic statement. As such, it constitutes not a proposition with fixed content but a stimulus to thought, an invitation to reflection, whose content is not predetermined by the person who presents us with the symbol. In this it resembles the cross or the breaking of bread. The fact that the expression 'image of God' has functioned in this way is in keeping with its lack of explicitness in its context. By its nature Genesis 1:26–7 opens up fields for thought rather than circumscribing thought. In principle it thus legitimates the insights regarding human nature which have been expressed when people have stressed rationality, or morality, or spirituality, or control, or creativity, or bodiliness, or relationship. The description of us as made in God's image invites us to keep chewing over the question, 'What does it mean that we are like God?' Our present concern is to make sure that we include disabled people in the 'we'.

In doing that, I group my thoughts around the notions of task, of journey, of relationship, and of body.

1. Task

If the idea of being in God's image is cashed out in Genesis 1 itself, this most likely comes in God's declaration of intent in so creating us: 'Let us make humanity in our image, after our likeness; and let them have dominion'. Being like God means being able to control the world on God's behalf; this is the task for which God created humanity.[1]

According to the usual view, Genesis 1 was composed among people transported from Israel to Babylon. They were living as a refugee community whose world had collapsed, and who had no control of their lives or their destinies. This creation story is told in such a way as to proclaim a gospel to them. One aspect of that preaching is the declaration that, against all appearances, God intends them to share in the control of the world and of life which God intended for all humanity. Against all appearances they are destined to share in power and authority. The fact that they are deprived of control of their lives, and are controlled by others, is not the last word, because it belies the creator's vision for humanity. In that vision an integral place is taken by the exercise of responsibility and stewardship, and thus of authority and power.

Now presumably all that is also true of disabled people, with at least two implications. First, it implies that the abled accept an obligation of seeking to share with the disabled the task of making the world, and the responsibility of exercising control and authority in the world. One aspect of this obligation is our vocation to seek to free the disabled so that they can control their own lives as we can – to help them be free, rather than to run their lives for them. In the context of modernity, the notion of sovereignty or control recalls that of self-transcendence – the idea that humanity makes the world and even makes itself. The idea that humanity makes the world resonates

naturally enough with Genesis 1, for if there is one evident characteristic of the God in whose image we are created, it is that this God
is creator; so it is natural for us to see creativity, world-making, as a
characteristic of humanity, and a characteristic in which disabled
people thus share.

Second, the presence of the disabled among those who are in
God's image implies that the abled learn from the disabled how to go
about creativity, world-making, control, authority, as well as vice
versa. It has become a commonplace to blame Genesis 1:26 for the
spoiling of the world by a humanity which believed it had the right
to do what it liked with it. The text itself, though, has implications
which work in another direction. If humanity is commissioned to
rule the world on God's behalf and as God-like, its ruling will reflect
God's activity and nature. The story has already shown this activity
and nature to be of a generous and liberating, rather than a grasping
and oppressive, character. Beyond that, the disabled have the
capacity to reveal to humanity a facet of being human from which
the abled can often hide – that is, our weakness, vulnerability, and
dependence. It is only modernity, which has exploited the earth on
the gargantuan scale that threatens its very survival, which implies
that the key factor was something other than the text of Genesis
written 2,500 years ago. This key factor is more likely modernity's
re-visioning man as omnipotent, in the image of God who had
already been re-visioned as having omnipotence as his key attribute[2]
(the gender-specific 'man' and 'his' are appropriate). If the disabled
are characterised by vulnerability and the capacity to call forth love,
they embody aspects of humanity which reflect aspects of the being
of God, Father, Son, and Holy Spirit – aspects of the nature of
God which humanity is called to image in its controlling of the
earth. They embody the fact that there is sometimes a mysterious
power in poverty, vulnerability, and weakness – a power to move and
transform.

As people who are called to rule, people who are God-like, we are
insufficient for the demands that life places upon us, and we need to
own this if we are to rule in a way that is not ruined by it. We need
to prove that it is not only being Christian that depends upon trust –

that is, we are justified by faith; being human itself depends upon trust. We *live* by faith, by depending on something outside ourselves – God or an idol.[3] The disabled embody that fact about being human. We cannot be self-sufficient in relation to other human beings, or in relation to God.

The disabled also draw our attention to the fact that the attempt to exercise control, the activity of creation, occupies six days but not seven. Further, it does not constitute the climax of creation's story. The climax lies in a rest from activity, such as the disabled may be constrained to accept. But then they give us the opportunity to prove that 'only those who live slowly get more out life'.[4] They invite us to a patient, listening attentiveness which replaces decisiveness and competitiveness, and offers us transformation.[5] They invite us to the play, spontaneity, and impulse which are part of being human.

On the sixth day, then, humanity is created in the image of God the worker, the creator. On the seventh day God rests, and suggests another aspect of deity which this image will reflect. If disabled people need to be freed to take a share in the stewardship of the world which is involved in creativity, in the image of God the worker, the converse is that they can already model for us the possibility of being human and God-like by inactivity, not only by activity. Many disabled people are seeking to live ordinary lives in unconventional bodies;[6] perhaps they refuse to accept the fact that they are different. But others are people who live non-standard lives in their non-standard bodies – lives that are less active and more like a Sabbath without a week's work.

2. Journey

If we thought we could tie down what it meant to be in God's image, this would be a worrying situation. It would seem to imply that we knew what God was like. This leads into a second reason for our being open to 'thick' understandings of the divine image, under-standings that go beyond what may be justified by a historical exegesis of Genesis 1:26–7. What that statement means is cashed out over many succeeding pages of Scripture. When we meet with

God at the beginning of the Bible story, we meet with all of God, as we meet with all of a human being when we first meet them. Yet the more we hear a person's story, the more we understand them. The initial impression gets filled out – occasionally corrected, no doubt – but more predominantly deepened. So it is with the story of God.

A key point is God's appearance to Moses when Moses asks who God is. Moses is told, ' "I am who I am" ', and informed that God's actual name is 'Yahweh' (Exod. 3:14–15). One of our instincts in relating to disabled people is to call them by name; the name encapsulates the mysterious, treasured individuality of the person.

It is no coincidence that the statement, 'I am who I am', is as disputed and as enigmatic as the phrase, 'in God's image'. But it points to one insight: the fact that God is who God is as I am who I am – a unique individual who cannot be summed up by a list of characteristics. In later contexts, God is prepared to provide such a list (classically, that God is merciful, gracious, patient, committed, faithful, forgiving, though prepared to be tough: e.g. Exod. 34:6–7). But the list does not capture the person.

As a human being I can be described by means of a list of characteristics – such as enthusiastic, imaginative, colourful, physical and unassuming (some of the more repeatable adjectives which my friends have suggested). Yet such lists do not satisfactorily sum up the person. In a strange sense the fact that I am 'John Goldingay' says more about me than a list of adjectives does. In Euro-American cultures, names do not have the meaning they have in some traditional cultures: they do not express someone's destiny or God's promise to them. Yet they have just as much reference, because my name refers distinctively to that unique configuration of characteristics (both attractive and quirky) which comprises me. When someone who knows me addresses me as 'John', it can be a reminder of all that – and thus it is a precious experience to be addressed by name by someone who loves me. I am acknowledged as who I am, even if neither speaker nor addressee knows all of what that is. As a human being I am a person called by name – by God, and by another human being. In addressing disabled people by name, we affirm to them *that* they are and *who* they are. We affirm our love for them, which operates despite, or because, of the fact that neither we nor they may yet know much of who they are. Naming *reflects* knowing and loving – but at least as much it *expresses* loving and thus facilitates knowing. Somehow this has implications for people, such as those with Alzheimer's disease, who may be so profoundly mentally disabled that we may wonder what their 'knowing' of themselves can mean. 'They may no longer "know" who they are, but the Church knows who they are'.[7] It may often be apparent that addressing them by name is received as an affirmation of love which meets with a response of love and trust. The one who names thus receives, in return, the gift of being loved and trusted, and is built up.

So in Exodus 3:15 it is suggestive that as well as saying 'I am who I am', God offers Moses the name 'Yahweh'. Etymologically there is a hint that this name recalls the 'I am who I am', but it is at least as significant that Yahweh simply has a name and discloses it. The very fact of God's having a name draws attention to a unique individuality, an aspect of the one whom humanity images. And if there is a mystery about the unique individuality of each individual human person, how much more is there a mystery about the unique individuality of God.

The lives of disabled people also illustrate that part of the mystery of human individuality is its not being static and unchanging. Their lives are manifestly journeys. When a disabled person who has been neglected or institutionalised comes to be befriended and known, that person can change and grow. When a person becomes disabled, that takes them on to another journey which can look (and probably is) more painful, but which can also involve breathtaking transformation. The former may be led from bondage to freedom; the latter may look as if they are on the way from freedom to bondage – but may be able to take control of, or to own, their changing humanity in such a way as to make it a new form of freedom.

God's 'I am who I am' points to the freedom of God which makes it possible for God to be whatever God wishes or needs to be. It also makes God the origin of, and the model for, the freedom of humanity made in that image. Freedom, 'creative freedom', is the 'conscious, rational, discriminating, unifying, purposeful element in the human being that leads us in one direction rather than another'.[8]

In that context God's disclosure also hints at a key feature of the way in which this freedom is exercised. God's being 'I am . . .' is a promise to Moses – a promise about God's being one who will always be there, there when needed, there when a crisis comes. It is not a statement about abstract being – as the Greek equivalent, *ego eimi*, probably is – but a statement about a consistent yet changing presence. Who God is emerges in contexts where God is needed – contexts where other persons are in need and God becomes something new, or gives expression to something new from the depths of that inexhaustibly-resourced mystery and freedom, in a way called forth by the context and by the other person. For God and for human beings, the realm of freedom consists of possibilities not yet realised; our humanity is then actualised only contextually.

Freedom and the reality of possibilities not yet actualised are thus other aspects of being in God's image, into which the disabled may have spectacular opportunity to enter. The point may emerge in its own way from the story of Adam and Eve in Genesis 2. They are surely created with maturity as their destiny, rather than as being already perfect. Further, as human beings we are strangely capable of reflecting on who we are and thus of changing who we are and how we act.[9]

Yet one fact which the subsequent Bible story certainly reflects is that humanity is *not* God-like, however we understand the term. God-likeness is humanity's destiny, the goal of its journey; indeed, becoming human is the goal of our journey. Paradoxically, one of the things which then becomes constitutive of our being human is the fact that we are on the way to this goal which is at the moment unreached.[10]

When I was 20 or 25, I subconsciously assumed, I think, that now I was grown-up, nothing else much would happen to me; I was shaped, and the rest of my life would be more of the same. One of my slightly astonished reflections on passing 50 a few years ago was that nothing could have been further from the truth; and one of my excitements was to realise that there was no reason why a process of change and growth should not continue for another 25 years – unless death intervened, but then that is but a paradigm shift of change and growth. I was sad to read recently a novelist's observation that he has to do more research for his novels now he is 60 because he does not have so much new experience to treat as a resource. I was then encouraged to hear a theologian reveal that in his sixties he has carried on having all manner of new experiences which have become a resource for his theological reflection. The disabled both point to this change and growth in themselves and enable it in others.

Our lives are journeys. This may not exactly mean that they are progressing towards some goal, as if ideally we could reach that goal and then be ready to die. They may be more like individual equivalents of history itself: history manifests no progress (except in the trivial technological sense), but it constitutes humanity's journey, in which achievements and insights come and go, sometimes becoming platforms for new insights and achievements, sometimes giving way to failures and blindnesses.

The story of Israel's ancestors on their journey is a parable indicating that all humanity is on a journey. The journey motif does not reappear in stories such as those of Saul and David – though they continue to embody (or to stimulate) reflection on the mystery of what it means to be human. Both these kings are interesting not primarily because they were kings, but because this leads to the telling of their human lives, both of which (ironically) were characterised as much by constraint as by freedom – constraints from outside in the case of Saul (pulled this way and that by the Yahweh who cannot be understood), and constraints from inside in the case of David (pulled this way and that by the inner personality that cannot be understood).

If our lives are journeys, our reflection on them will naturally take such narrative form. That is true for disabled people – their problem being that they may have difficulty telling their story. Jean Vanier speaks of one of the first disabled people he lived with, a man who had not been told that his mother had died. In due course, Jean took him to her grave, upon which the man cast himself in sobbing anguish. No doubt that reflected the pain of losing his mother such as anyone might feel, and the pain of not having been told.[11] I wonder whether another significance of his anguish was that his mother represented his story, his past, his journey: he was now cut off from it and unable to articulate it; he had lost his history, his story, his 'memory'; he became in this sense a non-person. There is no doubt that disabled people live narrative lives, that their lives are journeys, but these lives' narrative significance may not become a reality for people themselves until they have the opportunity to articulate their story.

Because the abled are the statistical norm, we may think that we define real normality, and we may thus assume that we represent full humanity and creativity. Disabled people minister to us by making more obvious this truth which applies to us all – that we have not arrived. Full humanity lies ahead of us, in the resurrection of the body which transforms the whole person so as to make us fully human; and in the little experiences we have now, the little steps that we take, towards full humanity, as the Holy Spirit has God's way with us and brings about some anticipation of resurrection fullness. The disabled draw our attention to the fact that all of us are on the way to full humanity.

In so far as the journey is a corporate one, the disabled are simply part of humanity's journey, the Church's journey, their family's journey, my journey. They not only take part in that journey, but form a resource for others on it; for the question whether we are becoming human, growing towards imaging God, is in part a question about whether disabled and abled are journeying more and more closely together.

3. Relationship

Disabled people thus draw our attention to the fact that human beings are designed to live in relationship. They may sometimes do that negatively, by their unhappiness and frustration at not being in relationship. They certainly do it positively, by their uninhibited joy in relationships, by their lack of self-sufficiency which makes them more evidently need to be in relationship in order to live at all, and by their capacity to draw others into relationship.

After describing human beings as having been given control of creation, Genesis draws attention to the fact that they are created male and female. At least three possible implications of this fact are worth noting.

First, God goes on to commission them to procreate, to fill the world, and this has been reckoned to be the point of their being male and female. Yet on the previous day other creatures were commissioned to procreate and fill the world without such reference to their sexual differentiation (Gen. 1:22), and this makes it unlikely that procreation is the main point of the reference to human sexual differentiation. In many cultures, having children is felt to be a mark of being fully human, both for men and women. For many disabled people, having children may be an impossibility. They thus can help us to handle the question of whether full humanness depends on that experience. Humanity as a whole has, in any case, well kept the commission to fill the world, and may have to resist the temptation any more to overfill it. Disabled people may be compelled to discover, and to reveal to the rest of humanity, that there are other forms of fecundity, of 'capacity to touch hearts and to give life'.[12]

Second, sexual differentiation epitomises the differentiation and diversity among human beings. We have noted that it is the glory and the challenge of humanity that we are different from each other, and our gender is the most elemental difference. When men and women live, work, and worship together, humanity is represented in its fullness and God is imaged. When abled and disabled live, work, and worship together, humanity is represented in its fullness and God is imaged.

Third, in the context of that differentiation we are indeed made to be in relationship. That is so for human beings made in God's image because it is true for God in the relationship between Father, Son, and Spirit. 'It is communion which makes things "be" '.[13] God is love in the sense that the Father is love, and reveals the fact by realising the threefold divine being. God thus issues in Son and Spirit, each of the three unique but realising their uniqueness in relationship rather than in egocentrism. Our divinisation (our realising the goal of becoming like God and thus being human) therefore consists in our participating in God's existence, having the same kind of personal life as God does. Our salvation consists in the survival of that personal life of love in relationship, despite all the pressures that assail it – including death itself. 'A particular being is "itself" – and not another one – because of its *uniqueness* which is established in *communion* and which renders a particular being unrepeatable as it forms part of a relational existence in which it is indispensable and irreplaceable', so that we come into being in communion and love.[14] While will, reason, self-understanding, and moral instinct are important aspects of what it means to be human, it is now a commonplace to note that these focuses of the Western tradition overemphasise the inner working of the individual. I know I exist not because I think, but because I am loved and I love. Conversely, fear threatens existence; indeed, if my reaching out to someone else meets rebuff, my existence is threatened in an absolute fashion.[15]

A further implication of God's having a name which symbolises God's unique individuality is that we should not try to identify the uniqueness of Father, Son, and Holy Spirit, any more than we should try to identify the uniqueness of the individual human being, because that can only tell us *what* the person is, not *who* the person is; it is to destroy the person's uniqueness and make him or her a classifiable entity. The person's real identity is recognised only in relationship.[16] As Yahweh's exchange with Moses suggests, this being is intrinsically a 'being with'. It is of the essence of the triune God that it is metaphysically impossible to 'be' without being in relationship. The same is true of human beings in God's image; it is not that we first exist and then relate.[17] Our humanity and our freedom are actualised contextually, not merely by means of individualistic acts of choice, but only in encounter with other people in acts of love and trust set in the context of relationships of understanding and shared life.[18] Who God is emerges in relationships.

This is hinted in God's 'I will be with you'; it is nearer to being explicit in God's chosen repeated self-description according to which, as well as being 'I am' and 'Yahweh', God is 'God of

Abraham, Isaac and Jacob' (Exod. 3:15). They are words Jesus later
cast at some smart-alec theologians who produced rationalist argu-
ments for questioning the possibility of resurrection (Mark 12:26–7).
He added the gloss, 'God is not God of the dead but of the living',
with the implication that when God enters into relationship with
someone, that infuses them with a life that cannot simply expire. If
the relationship was real, it cannot have died. Jesus' gloss is in
keeping with Exodus. God's being is identified by relationships,
involvements, and commitments to Abraham, Isaac and Jacob. The
being of those made in God's image is also identified in relationships, involvements, and commitments.

Disabled people, and our relationships with them, draw our attention to this fact. They themselves enter into a fuller humanity in
relationships, and they call us to the same destiny in our relationships
with them.

The reality to which we are here referring needs to be expressed
in terms of living in community as well as in terms of living in
relationship, for the two are not the same. I live in relationship as an
individual; being-in-community takes the matter further. Living in
community with disabled people gives both the abled and the disabled the possibility of realising their humanity by being drawn out
of their closed individual worlds (which the abled, at least, may
see as the means of safeguarding their humanity) into a shared
life in a network of relationships. This network transcends exclusive-
ness, and both embraces and is embraced by other people who are
different from us. That makes us alive, personal, human. Disabled
people have a strange power to call forth love, and thus both to call
forth humanity and to reveal the nature of divine love. When a
culture like that of the West is characterised by interrelated individualism, isolation, alienation, and homelessness, alternative
communities such as those of the abled and the disabled offer an
alternative culture to the collapsing one – an alternative culture
which can establish an alternative order.

It has naturally been customary to find differentiation in relationship expressed in marriage; but disabled people, who on average are
less likely to marry, are among the groups of human beings who draw

our attention to the fact that marriage is but one illustration of humanity's destiny to live in relationship. If the assumption that people will have children is one tyranny that hangs over humanity, another is the assumption that people will marry – and even more the assumption that the relationship between husband and wife will fulfil virtually all a couple's need of, or capacity for, relationship. Each person in a couple has the capacity and the need for other forms of love and friendship, and the disabled remind us of, and illustrate for us, the capacity and the need for such relationships of love and friendship. More specifically, if they are not involved in full sexual relationships, they help to relativise the importance of sexual relationships for us. There are other forms of loving friendship.

On gloomy days I am inclined to reflect that in some North Atlantic cultures it seems that men do not want to be in relationship, and women want to be in relationship only with other women. There are reasons for both phenomena. The disabled remind us of the point hinted at in Genesis 1 – that some of the most fruitful relationships involve differentiation. It can seem easier for men to relate to other men, or at least for women to relate to other women, for like to relate to like, for abled to relate to abled and avoid disabled, and in some ways perhaps for disabled to relate to disabled. At the day-centre for disabled people to which my wife once belonged, I was struck by the sense of community and relationship based in part on what people had in common. The 'differently abled' political correctness at least invites us to see that abled and disabled are human beings who need to be in relationship with each other in order to realise more of their full humanity in differentiation.

4. Body

Being human is an intrinsically bodily matter. Disabled people draw attention to this, paradoxically, because they have to battle with being bodily in ways that others do not, and this continually reminds them and us of their bodiliness.[19]

We have noted that discussion of the image of God has often focused on human characteristics such as rationality, or morality, or spirituality. If this discussion referred to bodiliness, it did so to affirm that likeness to God does not lie here, because God is spirit. Yet an image is usually a physical thing, and a natural way to understand humanity's being in God's image is to see it as signifying that we are the appropriate physical beings to represent God in the physical world. The commission to rule the world draws our attention to an ongoing feature of the story of humanity and of the people of God: that it is lived in the world, in the way that bodiliness makes possible.

The statement that human beings are made in God's image stands at the beginning of the story told through Old and New Testaments, and it both interprets this story and is interpreted by it. It is as if, during the Bible story, we are invited to keep reflecting, 'Now you need to remember that this is so because they are made in God's image'. The incarnation is a key point at which this invitation is issued. God had no logical difficulty about becoming a human being, because human beings were created in the beginning as just the kind of physical beings that God would be if God *were* a physical being. Indeed, God's becoming a human being makes more plausible the idea that God's image lies precisely in humanity's embodiedness, and not in a spiritual nature divorced from the body.

The fact that humanity is made in God's image not only provides something of the explanation of what happens as the story unfolds, but is also itself explained and given content by that story. At the end of the Bible story we are thus invited to conclude, 'So *that* is what it means to be made in God's image', and the incarnation will again illumine what that signifies.

According to John Zizioulas, human freedom is not the ability to make a decision, but the capacity to embrace incapacity, the capacity to turn weakness into strength by realising power in weakness.[20] Disabled people are forced to take the opportunity of finding the freedom which comes from embracing incapacity, and in so far as they do so, they embody for the rest of humanity that aspect of being human which we are not forced to confront and may thus avoid. In denying capacity, we too may find freedom and capacity. We may again consider an insight from the moment when God appears to

Moses and asserts a commitment to Israel. They are a weak people, bound and frustrated, groaning and crying in bondage. Initially God does nothing to alleviate their weakness, except to tell them to go and confront Pharaoh. Perhaps that is the way in which they find freedom, and thus realise the image of God before they actually leave Egypt, embracing their weakness and thus turning it into strength. In turn, the incarnation leads to the cross and the disabling of God, pointing the way to a distinctive kind of perfection or maturity which is more explicitly related to vulnerability and weakness.

At the beginning of the story, once humanity is outside the garden in Eden, there is more reference to sex, parenthood, and work (Gen. 4:1–2); then one of the first things Adam and Eve's children do is pray (vv. 3–4). The understanding of the divine image which sees it as lying in our spiritual nature, our capacity to relate to God, has not misconceived the Bible's assumptions about what it means to be human. Prayer is an intrinsic part of that, even when people have transgressed God's limits and found themselves cast out of God's garden. Disabled people may remind us that worship and prayer are not spiritual in such a way as not to be physical, bodily. Worship and prayer are not – necessarily or solely – refined matters of brain and rationality.

Within the Bible's own book of prayers, the first actual prayer is a wail (Ps. 3), and as such it reflects the character of human speech in its elemental nature, before it becomes a cooler matter of brain and reason – as we fantasise, at least.

> All our early speech is an inarticulate eloquence that gets us what we need to survive: food, warmth, comfort, love. We need help. We need another. We are not furnished, as the lower animals are, with instincts that get us through the life cycle with minimal help from others. We are unfinished creatures requiring complex and extensive assistance in every part of our being, and language is the means for getting it.[21]

Disabled adults are real adults, but they draw attention to an intrinsic feature of humanity which, in adulthood, we can evade as we cannot in childhood: that we are not designed to be self-sufficient. We begin in frailty and dependence, and end there; the disabled remind us of our ongoing frailty, from which maturity enables us to hide.[22] They may unselfconsciously draw attention to hopes, fears and longings which belong to all humanity, to the loss of the past, to fears of nothingness and longings for completeness, to agonisings and yearnings, to alienation from oneself, specifically from our bodies, from other people, from society, from the world, and from God, to frustration, deprivation, and loss. They may also draw attention to trustings and self-loves that are able to be relaxed, confident and laid-back, in spite of the insecurity of the present, which they are less free to evade by striving for false securities (e.g. in activism, do-gooding or entertainment) than are the abled.

The mention of language might at first seem further to disable the disabled, who may lack language. By virtue of not lacking bodies (indeed, by being more focused on bodies), the disabled do not lack body-language. They may indeed lack much informative and performative language, but they do not lack that elemental bodily language of relationship which all human beings use before they have words – the language of plea, protest, love, hope, gratitude, and recognition, which adults surrender to their own loss. The disabled enable us to lament and to praise. As the gift of speaking in tongues enables the tongues of speechless people to find expression, as also happens in the primal scream,[23] so in their scream the severely disabled voice the scream of humanity.

They draw our attention to human beings' ambivalent relationship to their bodies. Our bodies are neither merely the shell within which the true person is found, nor the precise embodiment of the person. There is something miraculous about the way in which in every human being, freedom, transcendence and rationality are conjoined with a material organism. Disabled people help us to avoid the universal tendency to take too grand a view of humanity by so exaggerating spirituality and rationality that we forget the material substrate; it is through the body that we experience sensation, emotion, desire and relationships.[24] Disabled people teach us to laugh and to cry; laughing and crying are boundary reactions, expressive rather than linguistic.[25] When we laugh, cry, make love, or give birth, we have to surrender to our bodies, to surrender control of our 'selves' to them.[26] Disabled people illustrate sharply this aspect of normal human experience which we may fear and avoid, thereby reducing ourselves to being less than human. Our ambivalent relationship with our bodies as human beings means we need to let them have their way if we are to be fully human.

The lack of spoken language is a terrible deprivation, one of the most terrible of deprivations, and one that may threaten the humanity of the disabled person more than any physical handicap. This is not only because it so inhibits communication, but also because it inhibits thought and reflection, for the possession of language plays a key role in making thought possible. The lack of language thus inhibits self-awareness and identity. In the narrow sense, that might be only an intellectual's perspective; but we also live in the context of a broader contemporary awareness that, 'if you haven't told the story you haven't really had the experience'.[27] So disabled people, like women whose story has not been told, may not have had the experience.

Alongside the possibility that disabled people may lack that developed capacity for reasoning which is so important to intellectuals, we must then put the fact that, nevertheless, we do not experience disabled, even speechless, people as sub-human, certainly no more so than (schizoid) intellectuals. Perhaps human nature and the image of God should be viewed in the light of Ludwig Wittgenstein's famous notion of family resemblances.[28] There are a number of features which tend to recur throughout the human 'family', but most human beings will manifest some and not others, and the possession or lack of one or another does not make or prevent someone belonging to the family.

Disabled people also thus remind us again that being human, being in God's image, is a corporate affair. To the corporateness of humanity's being in God's image, they bring some gifts, as intellectuals bring others – and none is to be despised. The points which Paul makes about the Church as the body of Christ apply also to the body of humanity. The unity of humanity lies not in being identical, but in shared and complementary diversity. The disabled contribute their gifts to this body, even if we have no right to insist that they themselves view their disability as a gift to them. We and they nevertheless recall that whatever parts we are inclined to view as weak and foolish-looking therefore possess particular glory and dignity (cf. 1 Cor. 12:22–4). Thus communities without disabled people are disabled communities: the world needs the awakening of the community of the abled and the disabled if it is to be human.[29] It is important for the sake of the disabled themselves that we are wary of talk of 'common human experience' which excludes their uncommon human experience.[30] But in addition, when the Church or the world marginalises disabled people, it disables and dehumanises itself.

13

A 'STRANGE' VOCATION

IAN COHEN

Ian Cohen sets out to explore the vocation of the person who is mentally disabled. He uses the biblical theme of the 'resident alien' (gēr in Hebrew) to bring out the likeness and difference of the stranger. The people of God had been aliens in the land of Egypt – they had the 'soul of the gēr'; *God shared this soul. The vocation of a person with mental disabilities is to embody the soul of the stranger, so imaging God. Thus relationship with anyone who has mental disabilities enhances our relationship with God, and their priestly vocation is recognised.*

> I'm not ashamed now of being able to say it – it is an antique word, and it's one that's easily scoffed at, but I do have a sense of *vocation*, and I will have it to the last second of my life.[1]

In this interview, shortly before his death, the remarkable playwright Dennis Potter spoke of his passion for writing. His use of the 'antique' word 'vocation' communicated a sense, shared with many others happy to use that word, of being unable to do anything else but fulfil his vocation. Sharpened by the obvious pain of the cancer which was ending his life, his gift of the word 'vocation' to his hearers gained a special power, seen in the context of the way in which his writing grappled with the human condition. For him, the human condition was not one divorced from religion. When he was quizzed as to whether he had any feeling that life might be eternal, and was reminded that he had said that he had never quite thrown off the idea of believing in God, and that it featured in a lot of his work,[2] he replied:

Religion has always been – I've said it before but it doesn't matter, I won't get many more chances to repeat myself – thank God, religion to me has always been the wound, not the bandage. I don't see the point of not acknowledging the pain and the misery and the grief of the world, and if you say, 'Ah, but God understands', or 'Through that you come to a greater appreciation', I then think: well you nasty old sod, if that's God, that's not God, that's not my God, that's not how I see God. I see God in us or with us, if I see God at all, as shreds and particles and rumours, some knowledge that we have, some feeling why we sing and dance and act, why we paint, why we love, why we make art.[3]

He went on to say: 'I have no means of knowing whether that "thereness" doesn't cling to what I call "me" '.[4]

The notion of God clinging intimately to us is powerful. I would maintain that we are prompted to see the exercise of vocation as the expression of this. It is the working out of our relationship with the rumour of God in us – through our knowledge, our feelings, our appreciation and our creativity. It is not something which is bolted on to us as human persons. It is what makes 'me' me.

It is the purpose of this paper to explore vocation, and claim it as the possession of those human persons who are mentally disabled. Many mentally able people see vocation as something for them to explore in their encounter with those mentally disabled. The vocation of the mentally disabled themselves is seldom considered.

The nature of personhood

Egbert Schroten, in his article 'What makes a person?',[5] presents us with a short theological commentary on the traditional Western concept of a person, which he feels has been significantly informed by Boethius' definition, 'A person is an individual substance of rational nature'.[6] From a theological view, he maintains that the defining characteristics of personhood are: createdness, subject-ivity, relations (qualified by love), vocation (*imago dei*, responsibility). A person is a fellow-subject in creation, called to an agapeistic way of life.[7] Schroten is concerned that these terms, and the words we use, should be more 'function words' than 'capacity words'. Thus on createdness he says: 'A human being is a creature among other creatures and is, as such, dependent on his or her Creator and surroundings'.[8] On 'subject-ivity' he says that the starting-point for discussion on the nature of personhood is not individuality but relation:

> We are created as fellow-human or, even better, as partner or neighbour. In biblical perspective no misunderstanding is possible about that: prior to anything else men and women are beings-in-relation. They have a relationship to God (in creation and covenant) to the other (in marriage and covenant), and to all their fellow creatures . . . They are what they are in relationship. In relationship they get their identity, a name, a face. That is why I, as a theologian, consider the word 'person' primarily to be a 'relation word'. That does not imply a denial of individuality, but individuality is what it is in relation to others.[9]

With that affirmation he sees each human being as a physical–spiritual unity; he sees each person as a 'subject'. On 'vocation' he says that rather than rationality (as Boethius saw it)[10] being a defining characteristic of a person, 'one would rather think of *imago dei*, a characteristic that might be interpreted in terms of being a partner in the covenant, answering God's call'.[11] To round it off Schroten says:

> What was said . . . about relationship may be qualified by the word 'love'. This qualification goes into two directions:
> (1) God loves his creation, especially his covenant-partners, and they may enjoy it; and
> (2) *imago dei* might be interpreted in terms of an agapeistic way of life.
>
> In other words we are objects of love and we are called to be subjects of love.[12]

Vocation is at the heart of what makes any person – those who are mentally disabled just as much as those who are mentally able. Furthermore, it is a function word rather than a capacity word: it has to do with our creation as persons in the image of God, whether we are mentally able or mentally disabled. However, it is when we consider those mentally disabled that we see the force of what Schroten says concerning 'rationality'. The characteristic of rationality is too limiting, and perhaps the characteristic of *imago dei* needs to reach out and include disability.

The biblical outsider

For some while now I have been reflecting on the meaning of mental disability, if I can describe it like that.[13] In this respect I have found the *gērim* of the Hebrew Bible (and the *paroikos* of the New Testament and the early Church) a helpful model for understanding mental disability.

A *gēr* (plural *gērim*) was a sojourner, or more technically a 'resident alien', who in the Hebrew Bible was 'a person living in a mutually responsible association with a community not originally his own, or in a place not inherently his own'.[14] He was a 'protected or dependent foreigner',[15] 'a protected stranger . . . of another tribe or district who, coming to sojourn in a place where he was not strengthened by the presence of his own kin, put himself under the protection of a clan, or of a powerful chief'.[16]

Throughout the Hebrew Bible, where the term *gēr* is used, it can be seen that the sojourner was very much a member of Israelite society, but a distinct member. He was distinct from the pure Israelite and distinct from the slave. But he was like the others in the community in so far as he was required to obey the Sabbath law and not work on that day (Exod. 20:10), but gain refreshment (Exod. 23:12). From such early texts it is significant to learn that the *gēr* was to be treated well and fairly, and protected against injustice and violence, because he reflected the 'true soul' of the Israelite as a person in relation to his God. He enabled the Israelite to 'recollect the feelings of the sojourner'.[17] Exodus 22:21 says, 'You shall not wrong a *gēr*, or be hard upon him; you were yourselves *gērim* in Egypt'; and Exodus 23:9, 'You shall not oppress the *gēr* for you know how it feels to be a *gēr*; you were *gērim* yourselves in Egypt'. Just treatment of the *gēr* goes to the very heart of being an Israelite, not because it was a fair or moral thing to do, but because of the 'function' that the *gērim* had in their fullness as people.[18]

The *gērim* were not, and could never become, 'true-born Israelites'. They were forever 'strangers', forever different. Later texts and later editors of the ancient material reinforced this view. When one comes to the character and way of life of the prophets, and in particular Jeremiah in his troubles and complaints, to live like the *gērim* and therefore reflect this 'true soul' becomes a key notion. Not only that, but we can see one sign in Jeremiah that the true nature of God was to be found in God living as a *gēr* – 'must *he* be a stranger in the land?' asks Jeremiah, requiring the answer 'Yes'.[19]

Looking at the New Testament, I have also previously sought to demonstrate that Jesus may well have made the link between the *gēr* of the Hebrew Bible and himself.[20] The three main passages in the Psalms which make reference to the *gēr* all seem to have a significant relation to the life of Jesus.[21]

The early Church perhaps extended this, and thought of Jesus as *gēr*. Matthew's story of the escape into Egypt (Matt. 2:13–23), linking with Hosea 11:1, makes Jesus clearly a *gēr* in Egypt. Luke's story of the birth of Jesus contains within it the notion that Jesus was a stranger who found lodgings in the manger. When this can be linked (a link not often made) with Jeremiah 14:8 – 'Why are you like an alien in the land, like a traveller who stays in lodgings?',[22] the picture becomes clearer. A key text for me, Luke 24:18, 'Σὺ μόνος παροικεῖς Ἰερουσαλήμ', can be translated, after Bauer,[23] in a way which also permits this link between *gēr* and Jesus in the mind of the author. It becomes a rhetorical question, 'Are you alone sojourning in Jerusalem?', and the Lukan style then requires the answer, 'Yes'. Luke thus makes Jesus the only true sojourner in Jerusalem, in spite of all the many pilgrims who must have been there for the Passover.

The early Church clearly identified itself as the *paroikos*, the Greek equivalent of *gēr*. The Church was the new Israel, and was therefore a nation of sojourners who lived as citizens of God's household.[24] They were not of this world, but lived in it. The people of God were *gērim* who were protected by God. Whether in their ancient or recent history, in Jesus, the people knew God to be *gēr*, with whom they shared a soul.

The linking of those mentally disabled with the model of the *gērim* helped me towards the possibility of getting deeper into what might be called the meaning of mental disability. It is in understanding the *gērim* as reflecting the true soul of God's people, even of God himself, that the link with vocation is made. Again, vocation is not some bolt-on aspect, to be donned like a certain set of clothes even at baptism. It is perhaps the *gēr* in our very selves which we must touch in order to understand ourselves. Those mentally disabled, like those mentally able, demonstrate this, but perhaps more effectively.[25]

It is here that I should like to add a brief mention of vocation as it is expressed within the New Testament.

The crying and the calling

Growing from the thinking within the Hebrew Bible, perhaps it is helpful to reflect on what we see there in the background: that *boao* – to call, to cry – contains within it the human person's expression of need towards God. Indeed, as Stauffer says: 'Biblical crying finds its deepest expression in prayer for God himself, and this leads to a new relationship with God. Prayer is elemental crying. It is the "mortal cry" of a being and it does not ring out in the void.'[26] Thus when the *gēr* in Deuteronomy 24:14f. cries out to the Lord, it is an indication that his call for justice is an intended characteristic of creation. It is almost a reflection of the function of the *gērim*, to call for justice – a call that had been Israel's while in Egypt – and this is implicit in the rest of Deuteronomy 24. It is a characteristic which is not dependent upon rationality either, for as Job completes his cry of complaint, his call upon God, he knows that even the land can cry out, and the furrows can weep over their concern for failing to reflect the *imago dei* within creation.[27] Is this not the 'eternal cry of the clay', as

Boethius presented it? 'It is the eternal cry of the clay to the potter, "Why hast Thou made me thus?" He will translate it, and after many days he will translate the answer, which is no answer in logic, but in excess of light.'[28] If anything might be described as the *imago dei*, it is not an answer in logic, but perhaps an answer 'in excess of light', like the illumination of Dennis Potter's sense of vocation.

Within the thinking of the New Testament, the word *boao* gives way significantly to the very much more common *kaleo* – to call, especially as in 'to name' – and thence to *klesis*. God's *klesis* is his call or calling, and this is what Christians are to consider (as in 1 Corinthians 1:26f.). Furthermore, they are to remain in the state of their 'calling'[29] which is embraced by hope[30] – even though, for some, their foolishness and weakness would be maintained. The functional content of this word comes to include other character-istics: of election, of being named, of appealing in prayer perhaps for justice; and, most significantly, there is the inclusion of the notion of 'assembly' in the use of *ekklesia*. God assembles all those 'holy', who belong to him. *Ekklesia* is a qualitative term, the assembly of those whom God himself gathers.[31] In the early Church, each assembly, wherever it was 'sojourning', was *the* assembly. K. L. Schmidt writes about *ekklesia* in the New Testament: 'The church, as the individual congregation representing the whole, is always visible, and its righteousness and holiness are always imputed through faith . . . The ideal is not to be played off against the reality, no more is the whole church against the local congregation. Every congregation represents the whole church.'[32]

From these initial reflections, I should like to emphasise the fol-lowing: the notion of the strong link between *gēr* as a model for understanding mental disability, and the *imago dei* as vocation for those who are mentally disabled as well as everyone else. Voca-tion is the *imago dei* within a person because of the soul shared between a person and his/her creator God, which is there to be embraced. Vocation is the function of each person as a subject of love – and not only an object of love within an agapeistic community. There is a significant strength in the way in which this is lived by those who are mentally disabled: their way of life is profoundly 'strange'. Such living is not a demonstration of human capacity, nor of capability – but one which is, of its nature, a demonstration of identity. This identity may have mediatory aspects – especially those whereby the 'soul of God' might be better demonstrated or experienced – but primarily is one which reflects a vocation as a 'sojourner' within the whole assembly of humanity. This vocation is one which is being lived now, but is also one which is becoming – one which many would describe as transforming.

Conversations of the soul

Michael Leunig, the Australian cartoonist, in the Introduction to his book of prayers, *A Common Prayer*, explains the meaning of his cartoon in which a man is simply kneeling before a duck.[33] He draws the man kneeling humbly in an attempt to talk with the duck. The upright stance is abandoned as a symbol of the laying aside of all that is 'able' in the man: power, stature, control, rationality, worldliness, pride and ego. He becomes more like the duck, seeking to improve his chances of communicating with it.

> The duck in the picture symbolises one thing and many things: nature, instinct, feeling, beauty, innocence, the primal, the non-rational and the mysterious unsayable; qualities we can easily attribute to a duck and qualities which, coincidentally and remarkably, we can easily attribute to the inner life of the kneeling man, to his spirit or his soul. The duck then, in this picture, can be seen as a symbol of the human spirit, and in wanting connection with his spirit it is a symbolic picture of a man searching for his soul.[34]

Leunig then goes on to describe how the person cannot actually see this 'soul' as he sees the duck, but he can feel its enormous impact on his life. Whereas its outward manifestations can be disturbing, dramatic and difficult to grasp, from its inner dimensions comes his love, fear, creative spark and even will to live. A strong relationship with this inner dimension leads to a good relationship with the world around him, whereas alienation from it, loss of spirit, seems to cause great misery and loneliness. The more the man comes to terms with this 'soul', the more his life takes on a sense of meaning.

> The search for the spirit leads to love and a better world, for him and for those around him. This personal act is also a social and political act because it affects so many people who may be connected to the searcher.[35]

If this is so from the stance of those mentally able, is it not also so when it is understood from the stance of those mentally disabled. The shared 'soul', which is common to the creator as to the whole created order, whether manifested in the *gērim*, those mentally disabled, or in the duck of Michael Leunig's cartoon, is characterised by the function of 'vocation'.[36]

This is perhaps true theology, emerging through 'conversation'[37] and the awareness of resonances that appear through that 'conversation'. It may be conversation with friends. It may be conversation with life (a duck?), or through encounters or experiences along the way. But in such 'conversation', resonances sound which for me have gained a coherence. On many occasions they have to do with what I might call the 'strange' vocation of those mentally disabled.

The 1994 Nobel Prizewinner for Literature, Kenzaburo Oe, writes perhaps somewhat autobiographically (being the father of a mentally disabled child) about the impact of the birth of such a child to 'the fat man':

> Later, looking back, he had the feeling that he had been counting on the birth of his child as a first step toward a new life for himself . . . But when the moment finally arrived and the fat man, painfully thin in those days, nervously questioned the doctor who emerged from the delivery room, he was told in an even voice that his child had been born with a grave defect. – Even if we operate, I'm afraid the infant will either die or be an idiot, one or the other.
>
> That instant, something inside the fat man irreparably broke. And the baby who was either to die or to be an idiot quickly elbowed out the breakage, as cancer destroys and then replaces

normal cells. In arranging for the operation the fat man dashed round so frantically that his own in those days still meagre body might well have broken down. His nervous system was like a chaos of numbness and hypersensitivity, an inflamed wound which had begun to heal but only in spots: fearfully he would touch places in himself and feel no pain at all; a moment later, when relief had lowered his guard, a scorching pain would make him rattle.[38]

The full impact was only later to be realised when experiencing another 'breakage' – when he was swung, by hoodlums, over the polar bear enclosure in a zoo he was visiting with his son 'Eeyore'. As a result of this experience, he was finally able to outgrow his madness, part of which was his dependency on his history. Between those two moments in this strange story, we learn of the fat man's intimate solidarity with his disabled child, believing himself to share the thoughts and senses of his child.

Until the decisive day when he was nearly thrown to a polar bear, the fat man had never failed to sleep with one arm extended toward his son's crib, which he had installed at the head of his bed . . . It had always been the fat man's intention that he was acting on a wholesome parental impulse – if his son should awaken in the middle of the night he would always be able to touch his father's fleshy hand in the darkness above his head. But now, when he examined them in light of the breakage which had resulted in himself when hoodlums had lifted him by his head and ankles and swung him back and forth as if to hurl him to the polar bear, eyeing him curiously from the pool below, the fat man could not help discovering, in even those details of his life, a certain incongruity, as if a few grains of sand had sifted into his socks. Wasn't it possible that he had slept with his arm outstretched so that the hand with which he groped in the darkness when uneasy dreams threatened him awake at night might encounter at once the comforting warmth of his son's hand?[39]

The functional aspect of the vocation of people with mental disability is frequently redemptive in this way, because through it the human soul knows that it is 'shared'.[40] Such vocation is like a hand reaching out for comfort. It is the reaching out of God's hand towards us, and our hand towards God. If this is so, how does the vocation of mentally disabled people, in particular, become apparent? It is again not a matter of demonstrating some capacity, but simply of 'being' in order that others might 'become'. The following was reported in September 1995, following the fall of Srebrenica in Bosnia–Herzegovina:

> One woman reported that several soldiers, one of whom struck her with the butt of a rifle, had attempted to separate her mentally retarded 17-year-old son from her. She was finally allowed to take him with her on to one of the buses after appealing to a BSA [Bosnian Serb Army] soldier who had been at school with him. This soldier accompanied them to the bus and told the driver not to stop or let anyone take her son off. She stated that she reached Kladanj without further incident.[41]

The aspect of vocation which comes to the fore here is one that enabled another to be part of an act of redemption, for at least one moment of his life. It would appear that the mentally disabled son communicated through his very self. Many mothers' pleadings at other times and other places no doubt fell on deaf ears – even as it is reported on behalf of those physically disabled. But the presence of the mentally disabled young man created a different response.

There is a great issue for us, if what I have sought to demonstrate has any impact: that we should endeavour to permit those who are mentally disabled to exercise their vocation. Not to do so is to mar the image of God in us all. Is there a way forward for us all, mentally able or disabled, to release this notion of vocation within ourselves?

Vocation – the image of God

To live such a vocation, or simply to be, can only happen in community. This is the force of our biblical examination. It was never good in the Hebrew Bible for one to be alone,[42] and it has been claimed that 'to be alone, to be separated from one's kind and live without contact with other men, that was the ultimate fear of Old Testament man'.[43] If such were the ultimate fear, one can see the extra force that this gives to the function of the *gērim* in Israelite society, and also the value of the vocation of the *gēr/paroikos* within the *ekklesia*.

Within the liturgy another dimension of the vocation of those who are mentally disabled is well expressed by Michael Law – although for me his comments are couched over-heavily in the terms of an able-minded observer:

> How 'uninhibited' they are. For example, to have a grown man hugging and kissing you can, to say the least, be disconcerting on your first encounter with the mentally handicapped. The 'kiss of peace' within the liturgy is quite normal . . . except that it is given spontaneously at any point in the service! There is a sense of warmth and genuine affection which the mentally handicapped give and they are not handicapped by our social restraints. Peter came up to me and said, 'We are mates', and gave me a bear hug which almost broke my ribs. During one service he said the prayer of consecration with me in a quiet reverent tone and then knelt down to receive communion. The mentally handicapped love to participate, and like Peter, are not concerned whether they have chosen the appropriate moment or not. The notion of priestly ministry was irrelevant to Peter; he just wanted to be with his mate.[44]

I would suggest that vocation, as the *imago dei*, sometimes communicates like poetry rather than prose. At its deepest and most lacking in capability, it perhaps communicates like the silences in pieces of music or the spaces architecture. Vocation as the *imago dei* communicates non-verbally, as do ceremonies. Thus the statement, 'the notion of priestly ministry was irrelevant', could not be further from the truth – indeed, the very opposite was being clearly demonstrated, as in many experiences of worship with those who are mentally disabled.

To put it even more simply, vocation, as the *imago dei*, communi-cates. R. S. Thomas, in his poem *Migrants*, writes:

> He is that great void
> we must enter, calling
> to one another on our way
> in the direction from which
> he blows. What matter
> if we should never arrive
> to breed or to winter
> in the climate of our conception?
>
> Enough we have been given wings
> and a needle in the mind
> to respond to his bleak north.
> There are times even at the Pole
> when he, too, pauses in his withdrawal,
> so that there is light there all night long.[45]

Perhaps the migrant – bird or human – is a sojourner in the air, who needs to recognise within the drawing-power of a God by whom our very personhood was conceived, who so shares his soul with us. We can reflect this by acknowledging vocation, the image of God within us. It is the mentally disabled who 'call to us on our way', showing us the direction in which we must travel. It is here, as in other moments, that the priestly aspect of the human vocation is in the *imago dei* which makes a person – priestly in the sense of reflecting God to the world. This reflection is not a capable activity practised by one who has the capacity to do so; rather it is the function of a person who is perceived and affirmed as a person by the assembly of those who acknowledge their sojourning state. The priestly state is not a godly state; it is more the state of unconditional waiting.

W. H. Vanstone must be mentioned here.[46] In his book, *The Stature of Waiting*, Vanstone makes the 'passion' everything: it is the 'passion' which truly images God in Jesus. The death of Jesus reflects the extent of the unconditionality with which Jesus was handed over.[47] Handing over unconditionally – the 'unconditional exposure . . . to whatever the hands of men should do to Him'[48] – is what imaging God is all about. It is then the manner of waiting, which is 'peculiarly intense and poignant',[49] which characterises personhood. Vocation is not a matter of ability or capacity, but is a matter of function. Although it is a tenet always at risk from 'able' Christians, ability is not a requirement for baptism, and neither is sharing in the Eucharist.

Stanley Hauerwas, in his paper 'The Church and the mentally handicapped – a continuing challenge to the imagination',[50] says that 'the "challenge" of being as well as caring for those called "mentally handicapped" is to prevent those who wish they never existed or would "just go away" from defining them as "the problem" of the mentally handicapped.'[51] He goes on to say that we should allow our imaginations to be challenged as to how to act with the mentally handicapped. Our imaginations must first be ordered by:

> something . . . determinative. For Christians, that something is both the story of who God has called us to be and our concrete attempts to faithfully embody that calling. For a community with such a self-understanding, imagination is not a power that somehow exists 'in the mind'; instead, it is a pointer to a community's constant willingness to expose itself to the innovations required by its convictions about who God is.[52]

He therefore goes on to appeal for, and promote, the notion of an imaginative community which is Christian. Such a community must acknowledge the world as it really is, not using the terms of a world which lacks imagination, but demanding that 'we must learn to live imaginatively, seeing what is not easily seen, if we are to faithfully embody the character of the God we worship'.[53] Within such a community the mentally disabled:

> remind us that their condition is the condition of us all in so far as we are faithful followers of Christ . . . They are the way we must learn to walk in the journey that God has given us called Kingdom. They are God's imagination, and to the extent we

become one with them, we become God's imagination for the world.[54]

The *imago dei* within us all, whether mentally able or disabled, reveals itself as vocation. This revelation is one of the imagination. It has a function whereby we are 'drawn towards', rather than a capacity which seeks to fulfil itself through achievement or the exercise of capability. The mentally disabled reflect the soul of God, and our conversation with God is greatly enhanced if we not only converse internally with the *gēr* within ourselves, but also externally, with those mentally disabled beyond ourselves. In the same way Israel was called to just such a 'conversation' with the *gērim*. It is in such conversation, in the calling of one to another, and the response of hearing rather than action, of the qualities of listening and waiting rather than judgement, that the *ekklesia* of all those who are called, whether mentally able or disabled, will discover its identity and vocation. The mentally disabled are perhaps the priests of this imagining. That is their 'strange' vocation.

14

THE CREATIVE PURPOSE
OF GOD

FRANCES YOUNG

*L'Arche challenges mistaken ideologies and reminds us of human vulner-
ability. Frances Young takes up themes that have recurred in earlier
contributions, specifically organising them around the question of God's
creative purpose. What is life about? What does the future hold? Is
Christianity really a vision of perfection? Taking cross and resurrection
seriously, she suggests that 'any picture of the kingdom, here or hereafter, is
distorted which has no place for the paradox that pain and joy, transcendence and limitation, co-exist', and that 'L'Arche is a place where the
kingdom is anticipated, and so its true nature is revealed'.*

'Christianity is not problem-solving but mystery-encountering.' My
aim here is to see if it is possible to formulate a theology from the
perspective of encounter with persons who have mental disabilities,
not beginning with this as a 'problem' but as a revealing and dis-
closing moment which generates new insight into the classic
Christian doctrine of creation. My thinking, which began as a
response to the first conference at L'Arche (in 1993), was further
focused by the need soon afterwards to preach a university sermon in
Exeter Cathedral, for which the lection was the story of human
creation in Genesis 2. It is perhaps instructive to begin with a review
of that sermon.

The role of humankind?

Given the context, it seemed appropriate to begin with the classic
modern question: 'Apes or angels? Creation or evolution?' I sug-

gested that, after more than 100 years, the debate had become really rather boring. I asked whether it wasn't a great irony that, since Darwin reduced the human species to monkeys, we human beings have gone so far over the top that we've virtually destroyed the planet and come to the brink of wiping ourselves out. Since we stopped daring to think we're angels, we've turned ourselves into God – convinced that we're autonomous, responsible only to our own individual sense of what is right and true. I suggested that, like post-modern architects, we should perhaps rediscover classical perspectives, the wisdom of the past. So instead of going over the boring Darwin debate again, we should direct our gaze back to ancient philosophies, ancient answers to the haunting question, 'What are we, the human species?'

I drew attention to the following biblical passage, using it to show that long before Darwin, it was fully recognised that human beings were part of the created order:

> I said in my heart with regard to human beings that God is testing them to show that they are but animals. For the fate of humans and the fate of animals is the same: as one dies, so dies the other. They all have the same breath, and humans have no advantage over the the animals; for all is vanity. All go to one place; all are from the dust, and all turn to dust again. Who knows whether the human spirit goes upward and the spirit of animals goes downward to the earth? (Eccles. 3. 18–22)

Such a recognition enables us to rediscover an enlarged perspective on ourselves and our life: nature, as a whole and in particular (take a tree, for example), is so much bigger, older, younger, than 'me'. In creation, however, there is fragility and vulnerability – indeed, of all species, the naked human is one of the most fragile and vulnerable.

Yet we have learned to cut down trees. A placard at the entry to the Wild Fowl Trust at Slimbridge, Gloucestershire, used to proclaim: 'Humanity is the most aggressive and destructive species on earth'. Rationality has enabled a physically frail creature to dominate. It was the ancient philosopher, Aristotle, who said: 'Man is a rational animal'. In Genesis 1, humanity is made king of creation, the one to have dominion over the fish of the sea, the birds of air, cattle, the wild animals of earth. This translation no doubt encouraged the explorers and exploiters of the early modern period – but in the ancient world a king was a shepherd, the protector of his people, and the Hebrew verb translated 'have dominion' actually means 'shepherding'. Domination is a distortion. But still ancient wisdom recognised that humankind was creation's crown.

The fifth-century bishop, Gregory of Nyssa, suggested that humanity was a 'microcosm' reflecting in its constitution the 'macrocosm', that is, the universe. And so human beings had a choice: to live like the beasts or to live like the angels. Rationality meant not the kind of aggressive dominance modernity has made it, but an opportunity to stretch the mind, discipline the self, for union with God, to collaborate with God as God's image and representative in the created order, bringing God's kingdom into being, tending God's garden. It's a pity that it has taken doom-watchers to remind us that an ecological perspective is what the wisdom of our tradition has always encouraged. We are part of the natural order, and the whole natural order is threatened when we cease to respect our place there, when we forget our fragility, littleness, weakness, in our desire to master rather than to shepherd.

At this point in the sermon I turned to the important role of persons with mental disabilities. They challenge the slogan which generated modernism: *cogito, ergo sum* (I think; therefore I am). We need the 'stranger' to hold up a mirror to ourselves. I suggested that persons limited in their capacity to learn and think not only reinforce what I had said about being part of the natural order, and therefore subject to its vulnerabilities and its mortality, but also enable a shift in values, away from individualism, dominance, competitiveness, to community, mutuality – a human ecology which has the potential to be 'angelic'. I spoke about L'Arche, and picked up some of the 'wise sayings' from our meeting, then very recent: 'We need to put our minds in our hearts'. 'I smile, therefore you are'. *'Moi-même tout seule pas capable'* ('Me alone can't do it'). I suggested that what really makes us human is our capacity to ask for help, and that challenges modern claims to autonomy. 'Community means you never suffer alone'. 'My saviour is the one who needs me'.

My general thesis, then, is that L'Arche ensures that mistaken ideologies are challenged, and the deeper truths of the Christian tradition are reclaimed. In taking up my subsequent reflections on God's purpose in creation and in developing ideas further here, I find myself needing to think about eschatology, about the end as well as the beginning. I write then of the creative purpose of God.

The theology of limit

Christianity has traditionally envisaged God's ultimate purpose in terms of the saved joining the angels in heaven, playing harps and flutes as they sing the praises of God. Peace and harmony is restored to the cosmos, the powers of evil having been overcome, and all sorrow and sighing taken away. Whatever we make of this picture, it conveys notions of perfection and resolution, the end of earthly tribulations and the transformation of earthly limitations. Presumably the tone-deaf are gifted with musical appreciation, crippled hands pluck strings, and everyone acquires a thousand tongues to sing their great Redeemer's praise.

We will return to that picture later, but I hope with a different perspective. For such a definition of God's creative purpose fails to encompass the present world, and leaves no room for the imperfect, whether in mind or body, or in moral and spiritual awareness. Before revisiting that traditional picture, we need to explore what has been called the 'theology of limit'.

In his study of parables, John Dominic Crossan[1] tells a story about a person sitting in a waiting-room who, to pass the time, places a plastic cup a certain distance away, and tries to throw coins into it. Three hours later when the train arrives, he's thrown the coin over 100 times, and landed it in the cup exactly once. If he'd got the coin in every time, there'd have been no point in the game. The game depends on limitation, and, 'you tolerate a higher, even a total, failure-rate more readily than you will tolerate a total or even high success-rate'. I was thinking about these things when someone told

me a reinforcing story. A fisherman died. On regaining consciousness, he found himself beside an ideal mountain-stream in Scotland,
thinking what a wonderful place it was, and if only he had his rod
and line. Someone came and said if he wanted to fish, there was
tackle available, and he could choose what he liked – the only condition was that, once he'd made up his mind about equipment and
location, he had to stick with it. So he chose the best tackle and the
best place at the stream-side. He cast, and immediately landed a fish
– wonderful! He cast again, and immediately landed another perfect
trout. When this happened a third time, he said, 'I'll go a bit further
upstream'. But he was reminded of the conditions. He blurted out,
'Can't you do what you like in heaven?' In other words, he wanted a
handicap – perfection was too much for him!

With that salutary tale, let us turn to the idea of God's kingdom.
New Testament studies have long contested the interpretation which
projects God's kingdom on to the heavens. The teaching of Jesus, it
is argued, must be seen in terms of its historical and social context.
The Jews were oppressed by yet another foreign power, the Romans.
Talk of God's kingdom must have carried political implications at a
time when zealots were plotting guerilla warfare to liberate the
people. 'Thy kingdom come' was a prayer looking for God's intervention to put everything right, to put all enemies beneath his feet.
Taken up in liberation theology, the promise of the kingdom
becomes a political goal, a Utopia: the oppressed and marginalised
are raised up, the mighty cast down from their thrones, the hungry
filled with good things and the rich sent empty away. The reversal of
fortune is a sign of the reformation of society. Political action is the
demand of the gospel.

That picture, however, cannot but exclude people marginalised by
disability. As Ian Cohen has pointed out, you can, at least in theory,
remove someone's economic poverty, but you cannot remove the
conditions which make persons with Down's syndrome what they
are – or, indeed, persons with cerebral palsy, or other conditions
arising from brain-damage or physical impairment. As long as social,
economic or political issues are all you take into account, Utopian
dreams are conceivable. But people like my son, Arthur, bring us face

to face with the limits of the human condition, and require us not only to reflect on the realities of limitation and to consider the meaning of the fact that revolutions never do create Utopia, but also to reread the Gospels.

We are, I think, taken down the required route by a remarkable poem, entitled *The Kingdom*, by R. S. Thomas:

> It's a long way off but inside it
> There are quite different things going on:
> Festivals at which the poor man
> Is king and the consumptive is
> Healed; mirrors in which the blind look
> At themselves and love looks at them
> Back; and industry is for mending
> The bent bones and the minds fractured
> By life. It's a long way off, but to get
> There takes no time and admission
> Is free, if you will purge yourself
> Of desire, and present yourself with
> Your need only and the simple offering
> Of your faith, green as a leaf.

Does he mean that the blind see or not? Does he mean that the kingdom is here, or not? Is it just a matter of reversal, of miracle cure? Or is it rather that, as at Lourdes, wheelchairs have priority? I think the paradox is to be embraced. Read in the light of this poem the Beatitudes, I suggest, may take on a different dimension, equally paradoxical:

> Blessed are the poor in spirit, for theirs is the kingdom of heaven.
> Blessed are those who mourn, for they will be comforted.
> Blessed are the meek, for they will inherit the earth.
> Blessed are those who hunger and thirst for righteousness, for they will be filled.
> Blessed are the merciful, for they will receive mercy.

Blessed are the pure in heart, for they will see God.

Blessed are the peacemakers, for they will be called the children of God.

Blessed are those who are persecuted for righteousness' sake, for theirs is the kingdom of heaven.

(Matt. 5.3–10)

It is significant, I believe, that the kingdom appears most frequently in the Gospel parables. In this century, New Testament scholarship has gone round and round the question of how to interpret the parables. One aspect of parables that has been highlighted in this process has been the fact that they were meant to provoke – to get a response, to stimulate crisis, to change minds. Crossan's study explores the function of parables in terms of bringing us to the 'edge of language and the limit of story' – they transform by subverting the comfortable world we think we inhabit, and bring us to the boundaries of human existence:

> What is the connection between these two points, the kingdom of God and the stories of Jesus? I would suggest that the connection is summed up in the maxim: Parables give God room. The parables are not historical allegories telling us how God acts with mankind; neither are they moral example-stories telling us how to act before God and towards one another. They are stories which shatter the deep structure of our accepted world . . . They remove our defences and make us vulnerable to God. It is only in such experiences that God can touch us, and only in such moments does the kingdom of God arrive.

Whether projected on to the heavens or turned into the Utopian dream of a political ideology, the kingdom is falsified by becoming comfortable and comforting. Conversion happens through shock, crisis and challenge, not through myths of perfection – perfection will cloy like the fisherman's heaven. The gospel message is more surely understood when we cease to dream of a magic wand putting the world to rights. The proper demand of persons with disabilities – that they should not be treated as 'miracle-fodder', but accepted as they are – is something that can open our eyes to the challenging demands for a shift of values which are paradoxically integral to the kingdom and the parables.

The upside-down kingdom

So what is being said? Human values are not divine values. 'My thoughts are not your thoughts, neither are my ways your ways, says the Lord' (Isa. 55:8). Human beings look for success, for fulfilment, for valuation in terms of the contribution they have made. But value is not something achieved, or even inherent: it is something given, something accorded to something or someone that is valued by someone else – the worth and dignity of each person is given by God.[2] In community, we make real that dignity and worth by valuing each other – but the grounds on which any and every person has value is God's decision to 'put his name there' (to borrow a phrase from Ezekiel). Above all, the incarnation bears witness to the presence of God in the midst of the 'limit' to which all human life tends. In God-forsakenness, in the absence of God, is supremely and paradoxically the presence of God, and the terminology of kingship is subverted when the story is told of a king who plays the part of a servant, and who is marginalised, rejected, stigmatised, judicially murdered.

The trouble is that that atoning perception which lies at the heart of Christian doctrine is so often itself subverted by viewing the resurrection as the magic solution (or *deus ex machina*), the reversal of fortune, the restoration of perfection, the end of limit. Resistance to that easy dream is empowered by the insight of a person with physical disabilities, Nancy Eiesland:

> In the resurrected Jesus Christ, they saw not the suffering servant for whom the last and most important word was tragedy and sin, but the disabled God who embodied both impaired hands and feet and pierced side and the *imago Dei*. Paradoxically, in the very act commonly understood as the transcendence of physical life, God is revealed as tangible, bearing the

representation of the body reshaped by injustice and sin into fullness of the Godhead.[3]

For Nancy Eiesland this symbol – Jesus Christ, the disabled God – has transformative power:

> The resurrected Jesus Christ, in presenting impaired hands and feet and side to be touched by frightened friends, alters the taboo of physical avoidance of disability. Jesus Christ the disabled God, is not a romanticized notion of 'overcomer' God. Instead here is God as survivor ... a simple, unself-pitying, honest body, for whom the limits of power are palpable but not tragic.

Surely this is an example of how living with impairment can produce insight into the depths of Christian theology, showing up distortions which turn it into ideologies of success, perfection and reversal. The cross shatters attempts to turn the kingdom into a Utopian programme, and the resurrection doesn't undo that. Kingdom values, we find, are nearer to being discovered at L'Arche than where human beings seem capable of challenging limitations and surpassing them.

Now if that is true in the here and now, in the between-time, might it not also be true of the beginning and the end. If models of human perfection misrepresent the creative purpose of God as revealed in kingdom, cross and resurrection, might they not also distort if projected back to creation and forward to eschaton? It is perhaps in following through that lead that I can see the greatest shift in my own thinking – from seeing Arthur's condition as a major reason for doubting the existence or goodness of a Creator God, to embracing it as revelatory of what the Christian tradition is really all about. Creation surely must be coherent with redemption through cross and resurrection, not in tension with it; and so must our ultimate destiny. For in God we live and move and have our being.

The nature of divine creativity

God's creativity has always been envisaged by analogy with human creativity, despite many attempts to suggest that human creativity is secondary to God's. The second-century bishop, Theophilus of Antioch, pictured God as a craftsman, the essential difference being that whereas human craftsmen need materials – wood, stone, clay, paint or whatever – God was so powerful he could create out of nothing. Little did Theophilus realise the significance of his own point – 'creation out of nothing' had the potential to invalidate his craftsman analogy. If God did not create out of the divine self, nor out of pre-existent matter, but out of nothing, as Tertullian would argue a generation later, then divine creativity must be of a character other than that of human creativity, which can only inadequately reflect the creative activity of God. If God creates out of nothing, then what is created is not God, yet contingent upon God for the miracle of its existence. Creation, like the cross, depends upon the paradoxical absence and presence of God – God within God-forsakenness.

It was the writings of the twentieth-century mystic, Simone Weil, which enabled me to see this: she suggested that divine creation is an act of abandonment. The point is that if God is infinite, then the only way anything can exist which is not God is by God withdrawing the divine self and allowing something to exist other than God – making space, as it were, for the nothing out of which something 'other' can come into existence. With God around, the miracle is that anything other than God exists at all. But if that 'other' exists because God has abandoned it, not only must 'limit' be part of its existential reality, but it must have been allowed self-determination, a certain autonomy – God cannot impose perfection on it. Impairment is inherent in any existence other than that of the divine Being itself.

The right analogy for God's creative activity, then, is not that of a craftsman or a builder, a potter or sculptor, producing a perfect edifice or a perfect work of art, which is entirely passive in the creator's hands; rather it is the father letting go, allowing the son to go to a far country, abandoning power over all that has come into existence, while waiting and encircling and enfolding it all in love.

I am reminded of Julian of Norwich, the medieval English mystic:

> And he showed me more, a little thing, the size of a hazelnut, on the palm of my hand, round like a ball. I looked at it thoughtfully and wondered, 'What is this?' And the answer came, 'It is all that is made'. I marvelled that it continued to exist and did not suddenly disintegrate; it was so small. And again my mind supplied the answer, 'It exists, both now and for ever, because God loves it.' In short, everything owes its existence to the love of God.

The presence of God, in whom we live and move and have our being, is real and yet found in God-forsakenness. God-forsakenness is not tragedy – it is the condition of our being, of our freedom, of the possibility of our selves and our world opening themselves up to God. The depth of that insight is embodied in the impaired bodies of people who live with disabilities. Without that witness, we are constantly tempted to dream of an impossibly perfect world from which this world is a disastrous fall. Fallenness has an element of truth in it – by sin we have most certainly compounded our limitations and our impairment. But in this modern world, we desperately need to rediscover the point that the thing that needs explaining is not what is wrong with the world, but the fact that the world exists at all, and that existence is itself a cause for wonderment.

The kingdom, present and future

So we turn back to Gregory of Nyssa – known as one of the first great mystics of the Christian tradition. In the fourth-century intellectual climate, mutability and passibility, along with mortality and corruptibility, were seen as major 'problems' connected with physicality, things from which humanity needed salvation. The great insight Gregory contributed was that mutability was the condition of advance towards Godlikeness, rather than the cause of a disastrous fall from perfection. To put it in our terms, impairment and limitation are required if humanity is to have potential, to be stretched towards ever higher goals. Gregory had some insight into the necessarily corporate and communal elements in that *epektasis* – a word borrowed from Paul (Phil. 3:13) and meaning 'straining forward to what lies ahead'.

And that brings us to eschatology. God's creative purpose is not the attainment of individual fulfilment, or indeed of static perfection which soon palls. One of the earliest attempts to construct a system of Christian theology (that of Origen) began with the notion of a perfect heaven in which all created beings were enjoying contemplation of God. But that perfect state had clearly come to an end – how? The solution was that these heavenly beings got literally 'fed up', overfull like a child tired of chocolate when it's had enough, satiated and bored with gazing on the divine. They needed a distraction, a sensation. Hence the fall from perfection and the creation of the material world as a school to train people for a return to heaven. Return to that heaven, however, would clearly be unstable. Gregory saw that static perfection was as uninviting as the fisherman's paradise. As Crossan puts it, 'Which do we prefer, comfort or courage? It may be necessary to make a choice'. For Gregory, the spiritual journey was infinite, for no finite being can ever reach the end of the riches of the knowledge of the infinite God. Perfection has to be seen in dynamic as well as corporate terms, and human limitation is essential to the process.

So to bring my argument to its goal: the kingdom of God in Christian tradition is both now and not yet, here and not here. Any picture of the kingdom, here or hereafter, is distorted which has no place for the paradox that pain and joy, transcendence and limitation, co-exist. It's in their intersection within community that true values and goals are realised, for cross and resurrection are at the heart of God's creative purpose, clues to the beginning and the end. L'Arche is a place where the kingdom is anticipated, and so its true nature is revealed. Of course, there is only one revelation in Christ, but so often in Christian history it gets distorted by being subsumed by human ideologies. We need places where the revelation is renewed by communities conformed to the pattern of Christ which illuminate the gospel tradition. Those places won't be Utopia – they will bear in their bodies the brokenness of Christ's body.

Nancy Eiesland's final chapter on the brokenness of the Church, whose calling is to be a communion of struggle, draws the threads together around the Lord's Table where discernment of the body of the disabled God is only possible through conversion. The climax is a liturgy which includes the prayer:

> We pray to you, the source of love in the world, the beginning of justice in history, the origin of peace on earth. You are God for us.
>
> **Remembering . . . the binds and bonds of your body. You create the space of encounter, the holiness of supping from another's cup, and the ambivalence of breaking.**

At our first meeting, Youakim Moubarac compared L'Arche to the desert experience; but that experience, for all its hardship and physical mortification, was also a place where people found the joy of the angels in heaven. And here we have found the place where the tone-deaf are gifted with musical appreciation, crippled hands pluck strings, and everyone acquires a thousand tongues to sing their great Redeemer's praise.

NOTES AND REFERENCES

2. Touching the depths – relationship with the poor

This communications workshop was facilitated by Gilles Le Cardinal. The text was translated by Brian Berg and edited for the author by Ben Nolan.

3. 'Do you love me?' – staying single for the kingdom

These extracts are translated from *M'aimes-tu?*, a L'Arche publication.

4. I can't say 'Jesus', but I love him

A L'Arche publication, translated by Mel Horne, 1996.

5. L'Arche: the community and its relation to society

1. Quoted in A. Giddens, *Central Problems in Social Theory*, Macmillan, 1979, p. 3.
2. C. Taylor, *The Ethics of Authenticity*, Harvard University Press, 1992.
3. C. Taylor, *Philosophy and the Human Sciences*, Cambridge University Press, 1985, p. 253.
4. J. Rawls, *A Theory of Justice*, Oxford University Press, 1971.
5. H. Arendt, *Between Past and Future*, Chicago University Press, 1962.
6. M. Gauchet, 'L'éxteriorité du social' in *Le libéralisme et la question de la justice social*, Cahiers du CREA No 4, Ecole Polytechnique, Paris, 1989, p. 241.
7. cf. M. Feher, 'Identités en évolution: individu, famille at communauté aux Etats-Unis', *Esprit*, June 1995.
8. cf. J. Sklar, 'The liberalism of fear', in N. L. Rosenblum (ed.) *Liberalism and the Moral Life*, Harvard University Press, 1991.
9. M. Weber, *Science as Vocation*.
10. *Homo aequalis*, Gallimard, 1977, pp. 13–14.

11. M. Sandel, *Liberalism and the Limits of Justice*, Cambridge University Press, 1982, pp. 55–6.
12. C. Taylor, *Philosophy and the Human Sciences*, pp. 250–1.
13. A. MacIntyre, 'Epistemological crises, dramatic narrative and the philosophy of science', *The Monist* 60, 1977, p. 461.
14. A. MacIntyre, *After Virtue*, Duckworth, 1985, pp. 218–19.
15. cf. R. S. Peters, 'Authority', in A. Quinton (ed.), *Political Philosophy*, Oxford University Press, 1967.
16. P-M. Delfieux, 'L'écart unifiant', *Communio* II, No 2, March 1977, pp. 19–27.
17. My understanding of this has been greatly helped by reading an (as yet) unpublished article by Jean Vanier, 'Evangeliser les pauvres et être évangelisé par eux dans L'Arche', 1995.

6. L'Arche and Jesus: what is the theology?

1. Tzvi Marx, *Halakha and Handicap: Jewish Law and Ethics on Disability*, Shalom Hartman Institute, 1992–3, p. 353.
2. A. M. (Donald) Allchin, *The Joy of Creation: an Anglican Meditation on the Place of Mary*, New City, 1993.

7. Alongside L'Arche

A paper given at an ecumenical colloquium organised by L'Arche, October 1993.

10. The sacraments in L'Arche

1. P. E. Moore and F. L. Cross (eds), *Anglicanism*, SPCK, 1951, p. 410.
2. W. J. Grisbrooke (ed.), *Anglican Liturgies of the Seventeenth and Eighteenth Centuries*, SPCK, 1958, p. 120.
3. Thomas Rattray, *Some Particular Instructions Concerning the Christian Covenant*, Pitsligo Press, Burntisland, 1854, p. 115.
4. Grisbrooke, p. 143.
5. Bobi Jones, quoted in A. M. Allchin, *Praise Above All: Discovering the Welsh Tradition*, University of Wales Press, 1991, p. 46.

11. Making the body whole: some questions about Scripture and impairment

The author's translations of the Bible have been used, unless otherwise indicated.

1. In the course of this essay, I am using the distinction between impairment and disability drawn up by people living impairment, and used by Disabled

Peoples International: **Impairment** is 'the lack of part of or all of a limb, or having a defective limb, organ, or mechanism of the body'. **Disability** is 'the loss or limitation of opportunities that prevents people who have impairments from taking part in the normal life of the community on an equal level with others due to physical and social barriers'. These definitions are key to interpreting impairment texts in Scripture. For example, one theme in this essay is that God gives and purposes impairment; in contrast, other passages show that God abhors disability: e.g. Deut. 27:18, Lev. 19:14, Prov. 31:8, Ezek. 34:4.

This form of the definitions is given in V. Finkelstein and S. French, 'Towards a psychology of disability', in J. Swain, *et al.*, (eds), *Disabling Barriers – Enabling Environments*, Sage Publications/Open University 1993, p. 28.

2. For the effects of the Enlightenment and the Industrial Revolution on people with impairments, see: V. Finkelstein, 'Disability and the helper/ helped relationship: an historical view', in A. Brechin, P. Liddiard, and J. Swain, (eds), *Handicap in a Social World*, Hodder & Stoughton/Open University, 1981; cf. A. T. Scull, *Museums Of Madness*, Penguin, 1979.

3. Recent publications surveying archaeological and written evidence, and giving detailed bibliographies: R. Garland, *The Eye Of The Beholder: Deformity and Disability in the Graeco-Roman World*, Duckworth, 1995; L. N. Magner, *A History of Medicine*, 1992; J. F. Nunn, *Ancient Egyptian Medicine*, 1996; C. Roberts and K. Manchester, *The Archaeology of Disease*, Sutton Publishing/Cornell University Press, 1995.

4. For example: H. H. Wilke, *Creating the Caring Congregation*, Abingdon Press, 1980, pp. 19–30; W. G. Monteith, *Disability: Faith and Acceptance*, Saint Andrew Press, 1987, pp. 25–31; N. L. Eiesland, *The Disabled God*, Abingdon Press, 1994, pp. 70–75.

5. H. Avalos, *Illness and Healthcare in the Ancient Near East*, Scholars Press, 1995, p. 129; also, p. 73: 'The testimonies of healing are remarkable in that very little explicit discussion of sin or immoral transgressions are associated with illness'. For a comparison across ancient Near Eastern cultures, ibid. pp. 408–10.

6. W. G. Plaut, *The Torah*, Union of American Hebrew Congregations, 1981, p. 408. cf. N. M. Sarna, *Exodus*, 1991, p. 21. Compare too the tradition of Gideon, where God deliberately reduces the army of the Israelites so that the defeat of the Midianites will be seen to be the Lord's victory (Judges 7:2); cf. David's defeat of Goliath (1 Sam. 17:47).

7. cf. 2 Cor. 8:9, Phil. 2:6–8. Paul speaks of this paradox as the core of his message: 1 Cor. 1:23, Gal. 6:14. The word Paul uses of Christ's coming to rest is unique in the New Testament – *episkēnōsē*. It links to passages in the Septuagint, such as Exodus 40:34, 'The cloud covered the tent [*skēnē*] of meeting, and the glory of the Lord filled the tabernacle [*skēnē*]'.

8. e.g., Isaiah 59:9f. The effect of blindness is seen as an appropriate punish-

ment for people who abuse their power: the blind are included amongst those abused by people in power – e.g. Deut 27:18; cf. Ps. 146:5–9, Prov. 31:8. Not blindness itself, but the effects of blindness, are several times given as God's punishment: e.g. Zeph. 1:17.

9. *Encyclopaedia Judaica*, Keter, 1972, vol. 4, pp. 1088f.
10. cf. Ps. 34:18, Isa. 66:2; Heb. 9:14, 7:26, 7:28.
11. e.g., forgiving sins: the paralysed man – Mark 2:3–12; working on the Sabbath: the man with the withered hand – Luke 6:6–11; Beelzebul: the men possessed by blind and mute demons – Matt. 12:22–4. In other ancient texts, when a human heals impairment – doing the impossible – it is taken as the person acting in the will and power of the gods, e.g. Vespasian (Tacitus, *Histories*, 4.81).

12. Being human

1. cf. H. W. Wolff, *Anthropology of the Old Testament*, SCM, 1975, pp. 159–65, 226–7; I. Hart, 'Genesis 1:1–2:3 as a prologue to the book of Genesis', *Tyndale Bulletin* 46, 1995, pp. 315–36.
2. J. Moltmann, 'Destruction and liberation of nature: ecological theology', lecture given at St John's College, Nottingham, Oct. 1995.
3. W. Pannenberg, *Anthropology in Theological Perspective* (trans.), Fortress, 1985.
4. J. Moltmann, 'On grief and consolation in modern society', lecture given at St John's College, Nottingham, Oct. 1995.
5. Jean Vanier, a talk in the context of 'A day with Jean Vanier', Cliff College, June 1995.
6. N. L. Eiesland, *The Disabled God*, Abingdon, 1994, p. 23.
7. S. Hauerwas, 'What could it mean for the Church to be Christ's body?', *Scottish Journal of Theology* 48, 1995, p. 10.
8. J. Macquarrie, *In Search of Humanity*, SCM, 1982, pp. 15, 38.
9. cf. J. Macquarrie, 'A theology of personal being', in A. Peacocke and G. Gillett (eds), *Persons and Personality*, Blackwell, 1987, pp. 172–9.
10. So J. G. Herder, according to Pannenberg, *Anthropology*, pp. 50, 60.
11. From 'A day with Jean Vanier'.
12. Jean Vanier, *Man and Woman He Made Them* (trans.), Darton, Longman and Todd, 1985.
13. J. Zizioulas, *Being as Communion*, Darton, Longman and Todd, 1985, p. 17.
14. J. Zizioulas, 'Human capacity and incapacity', *Scottish Journal of Theology* 28, 1975, p. 414.
15. cf. J. Aves, 'Persons in relation', in C. Schwöbel and C. E. Gunton (eds), *Persons, Divine and Human*, T. & T. Clark, 1991, p. 125.
16. J. Zizioulas, 'On being a person', in Schwöbel and Gunton, pp. 45–6.
17. J. Zizioulas, 'Human capacity and incapacity', p. 415.

18. W. Pannenberg, 'Speaking about God in the face of atheist criticism', in *Basic Questions in Theology*, vol. 3, SCM, 1993, pp. 111, 113.
19. Eiesland, p. 31.
20. J. Zizioulas, 'Human capacity and incapacity', p. 428.
21. E. H. Peterson, *Answering God*, Harper Collins, 1989, p. 35.
22. Jean Vanier, *Community and Growth*, Darton, Longman and Todd, 1979, pp. 64–5.
23. J. Moltmann, 'The charismatic variety of life', lecture given at St John's College, Nottingham, Oct. 1995.
24. Macquarrie, *In Search of Humanity*, pp. 47–58.
25. See H. Plessner, *Laughing and Crying*, Northwestern University Press, 1970.
26. Pannenberg, *Anthropology*, p. 82.
27. cf. H. Walton and S. Durber (eds), *Silence in Heaven*, SCM, 1994, p. 153.
28. See L. Wittgenstein, *Philosophical Investigations* (trans.), Macmillan, 1953, pp. 65–7.
29. J. Moltmann, 'The charismatic variety of life'.
30. Eiesland, p. 21.

13. A 'strange' vocation

1. *An Interview with Dennis Potter*, broadcast on 5 April 1994 on Channel 4, pp. 9f.
2. op. cit., p. 41 – words of the interviewer Melvyn Bragg.
3. op. cit., p. 6.
4. op. cit., p. 6.
5. Egbert Schroten, 'What makes a person?' *Theology* XCVII, no. 776.
6. Boethius, *Contra Eutychen et Nestorium* III, 5.
7. Schroten, p. 101.
8. op. cit., p. 100.
9. op. cit., p. 101.
10. cf. J. Mitchell-Innes, *God's Special People: Ministry with the 'Handicapped'*, Grove, 1995, p. 6. 'Human life is not primarily about intellectual ability. No doubt the image of God in humans is made up of more than one characteristic. Intellect is one and imagination and creativity others. But I would share the view expressed by Michael Miles (*Christianity and Mental Handicap*, CBRF 1978) that, above all, sharing God's image gives the ability to relate to God himself and to each other. This is a characteristic that is often very marked in those with learning difficulties. Some conditions involve an impairment of the ability to communicate, but it is rare that it is not there at all.'
11. Schroten, p. 101.
12. op. cit., p. 101.
13. I. Cohen, 'They . . . endure all disabilities as aliens', in Stephen Pattison

(ed.), *Mental Handicap, Theology and Pastoral Care*, paper delivered at the University of Birmingham, Department of Theology, Pastoral Studies conference 1986; and *The Eternal Cry of the Clay*, St George's House, Windsor Castle, July 1992.

14. *Interpreter's Dictionary of the Bible*: article on *Gēr*.
15. G. R. Driver, *Deuteronomy*, International Critical Commentary, p. 126.
16. op. cit., p. 126, quoting W. R. Smith.
17. op. cit., p. 126.
18. cf. D. E. Gowan, 'Wealth and poverty in the Old Testament', *Interpretation* XLI, No. 4, Oct. 1987, p. 352. 'Most of the motive clauses added to laws concerning the powerless [i.e. including the *gērim*] remind and persuade those with power that these are people like them, worthy of the same respect as they. The basis for that is partly their common humanity as they share the same feelings, but it is primarily because these people have dignity in the sight of Yahweh ... Deut. 10:18f. ... The essence of the attitude toward the powerless commended by the Old Testament is thus different from what is often associated with "charitable works" ... The Old Testament insists that in one sense every Israelite is among the needy, because Yahweh says, "the land is mine; for you are strangers and sojourners with me", Lev. 25:23.'
19. Jer. 14:8.
20. I. Cohen, 'They ... endure all disabilities as aliens' (a title drawn from The Epistle to Diognetus 5:5).
21. Ps. 39:12 links with Jesus' passion. Ps. 119:19 in the Septuagint links with Jesus as 'the sojourning one' (cf. Jer. 14:8). Ps. 146:5–9 (cf. Isa. 61:1f.) has clearly influenced Jesus' Galilee Manifesto announced in the Nazareth synagogue (Luke 4:16ff.).
22. cf. R. E. Brown, *An Adult at Christmas*, The Liturgical Press, 1978.
23. G. Kittel *et al.*, *Theological Dictionary of the New Testament* (trans.), vol. 5, 1967, p. 853.
24. e.g. 1 Pet. 2:11 and Epistle to Diognetus 5.
25. cf. the experience of many parents who would describe their reaction to the birth of a mentally disabled child as like that of having read the guidebooks and learned a few phrases, then having boarded a flight to take a holiday in Italy, but on arrival being greeted by signs which say 'Welcome to Holland' – not what one had planned. cf. also R. B. Steele, 'Accessibility of hospitality', *Stauros Notebook* vol. 13, no. 4, Christmas 1994, in which he writes about the alienation of the disabled: 'The disabled and their loved ones are constantly reminded that they are "strangers" – not "strangers in a foreign land", as the Bible calls travellers and resident aliens, but strangers in their own land, and thus strangers indeed!' I feel that his definition of *gērim* is too restricted because the *gērim* were to become 'strangers in their own land' even though they could never become trueborn Israelites. It is precisely that which is 'strange indeed'. He goes on to

say: 'The disabled and their families feel like aliens. The disabled are alienated because they really are different, painfully so, from "normal" folks. Their families are alienated by virtue of their disenchantment with cultural myths.' The issue of alienation from cultural myths is an exciting one which is perhaps reflected in a question raised in T. Heller, R. Markwardt, L. Rowitz and B. Farber, 'Adaption of Hispanic families to a member with mental retardation', *American Journal of Mental Retardation* vol. 99, No. 3, 1993, namely, 'To what extent do religious values and informal and formal support resources mediate the care-giving burden?' They reaffirmed the received wisdom that Hispanic communities, in their stress on reliance on the family, are better able to accept the member with a disability. Any 'care-giving burden' was thus reduced, particularly when religious values played a part. Thus they make the suggestion that religious values also are a key cultural factor in the acceptance of a relative with mental retardation.

26. E. Stauffer, in G. Kittel and G. Friedrich (eds) *Theological Dictionary of the New Testament*, abridged in one volume by G. W. Bromley, p. 108.

27. Job 31:38.

28. H. Waddell (trans.) *Poetry in the Dark Ages*, Constable, 1958, quoted in Cicely Saunders, *Beyond the Horizon*, Darton, Longman and Todd, 1990, p. 79. The question is asked again, perhaps more poignantly, in the title of Caroline Philips' book, '*Mummy, Why have I got Down's Syndrome?*', Lion, 1991.

29. 1 Cor. 7:20.

30. Eph. 1:18.

31. K. L. Schmidt in Kittel *et al.* p. 398.

32. op. cit., pp. 40f.

33. M. A. Leunig, *Common Prayer*, Lion, 1997.

34. op. cit., Introduction.

35. op cit., Introduction.

36. Rublev's icon of the Trinity can perhaps be explored with this in mind. Is it an icon of a 'soul' being shared, a conversation, in which all hear the call of one, in which God is calling to himself?

37. cf. M. Wiles, *A Shared Search: Doing Theology in Conversation with One's Friends*, SCM, 1994, p. 18: 'Theology is best done in [a] more tentative and exploratory manner in which the theologian tries to find a way through some of the difficulties of understanding and for practice that are encountered in the accepted forms of faith. One of the criteria that the vital appeal to reason imposes is the criterion of consistency . . . It is that necessity that fuels a drive in the direction of a more systematic theology. But if that is its motivation, then the kind of construction to which it points needs to be seen not so much as providing houses for the Church to dwell in, but rather as testing the consistency, and thereby the validity, of more particular theological reflections . . . Exploratory enquiry (itself serving the way of faith) is nearer to the heart of the matter. And that . . . needs to be pursued

not just in the isolation of the theologian's own private reflections but in active conversation with others.' Wiles chooses the word 'consistency', while I would prefer 'coherence' in my necessarily more tentative and meagre theological endeavours.

38. Kenzaburo Oe, *Teach us to Outgrow our Madness*, 1989, p. 176.
39. op. cit., p. 179.
40. cf. A. Cole, 'The disabled as prophets', *The Tablet*, 2 Sept. 1995, p. 1107. 'Down's children have been called the "gentle prophets" of our times. They are individuals who take each day as it comes and respond trustingly with a smile to a smile. Status, trappings and prestige mean nothing to them; they relate immediately and directly to the heart. They are generous and genuine, with a disconcerting ability to expose the weaknesses and prejudices of those around them. Their prophetic qualities redeem themselves and us – if we let them.'
41. *Bosnia–Herzegovina: The Missing of Srebrenica*, Amnesty International, Sept. 1995 (AI Index EUR 63/22/95).
42. Gen. 2:18.
43. G. A. F. Knight, *A Christian Theology of the Old Testament*, SCM, 1959, p. 27, quoted in J. Pragnell, 'Vision and reality: community care and mental handicap', *Hospital Chaplain*, Dec. 1987, p. 22.
44. M. Law, 'Worship with the mentally handicapped', *Hospital Chaplain*, Sept. 1986, pp. 7f.
45. R. S. Thomas, *Mass for Hard Times*, Bloodaxe, 1992, p. 80.
46. W. H. Vanstone, *The Stature of Waiting*, Darton, Longman and Todd, 1982.
47. op. cit., p. 78.
48. op. cit., p. 79.
49. op. cit., p. 84.
50. S. Hauerwas, *Dispatches from the Front*, Duke University Press, 1994, pp. 177ff.
51. op. cit., p. 177.
52. op. cit., pp. 179ff.
53. op. cit., p. 180.
54. op. cit., p. 185.

14. The creative purpose of God

1. John Dominic Crossan, *The Dark Interval: Towards a Theology of Story*, Polebridge Press, 1988.
2. David Pailin, *A Gentle Touch: From a Theology of Handicap to a Theology of Human Being*, SPCK, 1992.
3. Nancy Eiesland, *The Disabled God: Towards a Liberation Theology of Disability*, Abingdon Press, 1994.